SACRED WISDOM

PLATO'S REPUBLIC

A Vision of Truth, Justice,
and the Ideal Society

Abridged and Introduced by
Alan Jacobs

WATKINS PUBLISHING
LONDON

This edition produced in 2010 for Sacred Wisdom,
an imprint of Watkins Publishing
Sixth Floor, Castle House, 75–76 Wells Street, London W1T 3QH
Distributed in the United States and Canada by
Sterling Publishing Co., Inc.
387 Park Avenue South, New York, NY 10016-8810

First published in the UK in 2009

Copyright © Watkins Publishing,
a division of Duncan Baird Publishers 2009

Sacred Wisdom design copyright © Duncan Baird Publishers
Text abridgement copyright © Alan Jacobs
Introduction copyright © Alan Jacobs

1 3 5 7 9 10 8 6 4 2

Designed in Great Britain by Jerry Goldie
Printed and bound in India by Imago

Library of Congress Cataloging-in-Publication data available

ISBN: 978-1-906787-45-5

www.watkinspublishing.co.uk

CONTENTS

INTRODUCTION

The foundation translation of this seminal political work into English is undoubtedly the work of Thomas Taylor (1758–1835), universally acclaimed as 'Tom Taylor the Neo-Platonist'. He achieved the remarkable feat of being the first to translate the entire works of Plato and Aristotle in his lifetime. He had a strong influence on the great English poets such as Blake, Shelley and Wordsworth, and in America was highly praised by Ralph Waldo Emerson. His fine translation of *The Republic* took many years to perfect and was welcomed with enthusiastic appreciation by the English-speaking world. *The Republic* is considered by many authorities to be Plato's greatest work, and the synthesis of his thought to form a complete philosophy for man.

Plato was born in Athens in 428 BC to an Aristocratic family. In manhood he became a pupil of the Athenian cult figure and famed eccentric sage and philosopher, Socrates. After Socrates' death Plato devoted himself to continuing the work of his teacher. He founded the famous Academy in Athens, the first institution to serve as the model for a Western university.

It was at the Academy, around the year 380 BC, that Plato composed the work known popularly as *The Republic*, from its Latin title, '*Res Publica*', meaning 'public affairs'. It soon became one of the most influential philosophical works of political theory ever written, and Plato's best-known dialogue. In it, Socrates and various Athenian dignitaries discuss the important question 'What is the true meaning of justice?' and try to answer the vexed question of whether a just man is happier than an unjust man. To solve these dilemmas they constructed a Utopian city-state to be ruled by a Philosopher Guardian or King.

The noted British philosopher Bertrand Russell neatly divides the work into three parts: Books 1–5 are Utopian, portraying an ideal community and the beginning of an attempt to define the meaning of justice; Books 6–7 concentrate on what exactly is a Philosopher, seen as the ideal ruler of such a community; and Books 8–9 discuss the practical forms that the government of such a community should take.

After a great deal of interesting and provocative discussion about the idea of justice, in which Socrates skilfully refutes all the commonplace suggestions put to him, the conclusion is eventually reached that justice is the 'perfect harmony' that can be achieved in a well-structured society.

The soul, or essential Being, inherent in every human, has a threefold structure: the rational, which seeks after truth and wisdom and is responsible for a person's philosophical inclination; a spiritual part, which seeks an honourable, worthwhile life; and an appetitive part, which desires wealth to fulfil its wants, needs and ambitions. The truly 'just individual' is someone who achieves the perfect harmony in which the rational rules.

There then follow three inspired analogies: the allegories of the Sun, the Line, and the Cave. The analogy of the Sun illuminates the Form of the Good, the Philosopher King's ultimate goal. The Line illustrates the four different grades of cognitive or intelligible activity, the highest of which only the Philosopher Kings attain. But in the allegory of the Cave we have arguably one of the most profound metaphors ever conceived to describe the mystery of the human condition.

Briefly, Plato suggests the body is like a prison house in which the immortal soul is entrapped. The allegory of the Cave fully explains the essential difference between those who see only 'appearances' and those who are able to look beyond mere 'appearances' and know reality as it truly exists. The metaphor expresses the eternal conflict between the world of the senses and the world of intelligible ideas. It is the Philosopher's sacred task to be the mediator between these two, the empirical and the metaphysical.

Plato narrates the considerable well-argued discussions that took place concerning the question of what constitutes the Ideal State. There is also stringent criticism of lesser forms of government such as Timocracy, or persons elected simply for their degree of honourable reputation. Timocracy will lead to a gilded government valuing materialism above all else. Then there is Oligarchy, which is a dictatorship by the few to the detriment of the many. Our own Democracy comes in for criticism for causing tension between the social classes, and being fertile soil for the demagogue. Tyranny is of course the worst form of government, leading to cruelty and repression. In the Ideal State, government by the Guardian or Philosopher King is easily the best because he has been well educated to rule and is dedicated to the 'Form of the Good'.

Paradoxically, although Plato is considered by many to be a poetically inspired philosopher, he is critical of poetry in his form of education, which largely focuses on mathematics, music, dialectics and gymnastic prowess. Poetry, as a study on its own, could lead to undesirable social consequences, if it imitatively stirs up undesirable passions, instead of being devoted to its true vocation, which is spiritual. Book 3 has a great deal to say about controlling sexuality and the need to transmute physical passions into the pursuit of the Good.

A revolutionary proposal is for the children of both sexes to be educated equally and together, so that women can adopt political roles as well as men. Controversially in Book 5 we have the suggestion that spouses and children shall be held in common. Family life as we understand it is reserved for the Guardians. The Guardian or the Philosopher King is trained to possess gnosis and virtue, as only he is educated to know, understand and live the true 'Form of the Good'.

The book finally ends on a grand coda when Socrates relates Er's vision of the afterlife.

I have endeavoured to freely modernize and abridge this somewhat archaic text to the best of my ability, without losing any of Thomas Taylor's unique personal style, or Socrates' essential meaning, which has attracted so many important readers and literary figures to this seminal translation, over centuries.

This is only a brief introduction to a very readable, provocative and enjoyable book. One may thoroughly enjoy reading Socrates' discourse not only for its profound wisdom, metaphysical truth, and political insight, but also for his occasional bursts of comic irony which enliven the text. It is true to say that reading *The Republic* is a stimulating education in both philosophy and ethics. It is a firm foundation too for the study of political science. The main criticism that can be made is that it is far too utopian and idealistic to ever be put into practice, but as a literary and philosophical work of the first order, the book undoubtedly excels.

Alan Jacobs
London, May 2009

BOOK 1

THE MEANING OF JUSTICE

SPEAKERS:

SOCRATES   ADIMANTUS

GLAUCO   POLEMARCHUS

CEPHALUS   THRASYMACHUS

THE WHOLE BOOK IS A CONTINUOUS DISCOURSE
NARRATED BY SOCRATES

The Scene is in the House of Cephalus, at the Piraeus

I went down yesterday to Piraeus, with Glauco, the son of Aristo, to pay my devotions to the Goddess; and I wished, at the same time, to see how they would celebrate the festival, when Polemarchus, the son of Cephalus, ordered his boy to run and ask us to wait for him. Soon afterwards came Polemarchus, Adimantus the brother of Glauco, Niceratus the son of Nicias, and some other friends. 'Then,' said Polemarchus, 'come to my house after the festival, there will be a gathering of friends there for a convivial meeting.' 'Don't you see, how many there are of us?' said Glauco. 'Undoubtedly I do, but let me persuade you to come with us, in any case?' 'It seems better,' said Glauco, 'that we should all stay here for a while.' 'If you have made up your mind Glauco,' I said, 'then stay here we shall.'

Later on, all of us then walked over to Polemarchus's house, and there we found both Lysias and Euthydemus, brothers of Polemarchus, also Thrasymachus the Chalcedonian, Charmantides the Pæanian, and Clitopho the son of Aristonymus. Cephalus, the father of Polemarchus, was also in the house. He looked to me to be growing very old, for I had not seen him for a long, long time. Immediately, when Cephalus saw me, he hailed me. 'Truly,' I said, 'Cephalus, I take great pleasure in talking with those who are very far advanced in years, for it appears to me reasonable, that we should learn from them, as persons who have travelled life's journey before us. We should learn what the road is that we have to take, whether it is rough and difficult, or smooth and easy. So I would gladly learn from you, as you have now arrived at that time of life which the poets call the threshold of old age. What is your opinion of old age? Do you consider it to be a grievous part of life, or what do you believe it to be?'

'I will tell you, Socrates,' he said. Most of us, when we reach old age, regret our state, and feel a lack of the pleasures of youth, and remember the delights of making love, drinking, and feasting, and other joys like these, and express indignation, as we're deprived of such precious experiences. In those days, we lived, but now we do not live at all! Some of us, too, resent the contempt which old age meets with from their acquaintances, and for this reason they also dislike old age, which is to them the cause of so many ills.'

Being delighted to hear him say such things, and wishing for him to speak further, I encouraged him, and said, 'I think, Cephalus, the general population will not agree with you in what you say, but will imagine that you carry the burden of old age easily, not from your own will, but because you possess a great deal of wealth; for the rich, as they say, have many consolations. But tell me, what do you think is the greatest good that you have derived from the possession of much wealth?'

'Probably,' he said, 'which I shall not succeed in persuading the general population, is peace of mind. For rest assured, Socrates, that after a man begins to think he's soon going to die, he feels great fear and concern about many matters which did not disturb him before. All those stories concerning the future afterlife, which say that the man who has committed injustice here must be punished there, though he formerly ridiculed such an idea, now troubles his mind with fears that they may actually be true. And the same man either through the infirmity of old age, or approaching that state, views them more attentively, and he therefore becomes full of suspicion and dread. He considers and reviews whether he has, in any way, injured anyone unjustly. Then he finds in his life much to be ashamed of, and many a time he is awakened from sleep, just like children in fear. So he lives in wretched anticipation of doom. But the man who is unaware of committing any injustices still enjoys living in hope, which is the sweet amelioration of old age.'

'You speak most eloquently, Cephalus,' I replied. 'But with respect to this very question of justice. Whether we should call it simply the truthful restoring of what one man has received from another, or shall we say that the very same deeds may sometimes be done justly, and sometimes unjustly? My meaning is this, everyone would say, that if a man ever receives arms from his friend who was of a sound mind, it would not be right to give such weapons back, if he should demand them when he is now insane, neither would their restoration be just; nor would it be just to a man in such a condition to willingly tell him all the truth.

'Then, always to speak the truth, and give back what one has received, is that not the definition of justice?' 'It is not, Socrates,' replied Polemarchus, 'if at least we may give any credit to the opinions of Simonides.' 'However that may be, I retire from this argument, I must go,' said Cephalus smiling, and at the same time departed to attend the sacred rites.

'So for Polemarchus the just is good?' I said. 'Then, is it not the role of a just man to not hurt, either a friend or any other, but on the contrary, only to hurt the unjust man. But if anyone says that it is just to give everyone his due, and inwardly thinks that hurt is due to enemies from a just man, and profit to his friend, he is unwise who said so, for he does not speak the truth. For it has nowhere occurred to me that any just man should hurt anyone.'

Thrasymachus frequently, during our reasoning, had tried to interrupt in the middle of the conversation, to take control of the discourse. When we paused, he was no longer quiet. 'What trifling!' he exclaimed. 'Socrates? If you truly want to know what is just, don't only ask questions, nor content yourself in merely contradicting when anyone replies to you about anything, because it is easier for you to question rather than to answer, so you should answer yourself, and tell us what it is that you call just.'

'Thrasymachus,' I said, 'the advantage to the more powerful, I think you believe that is what is just.' 'You are most impudent, Socrates, and interpret my thoughts where you think you may do the greatest injury. This is what I maintain, Socrates, that, in all states, what is just, and what is advantageous for the established government, are the same because it wields the power. So that it appears to him who reasons rightly, that, in all cases, what is to the advantage of the more powerful is the just.'

'But Thrasymachus, no science of government or any other merely considers the advantage of the more powerful, nor approves of it, but rather favours the less powerful, that is those who are governed. No ruler, in any government, as far as he is the Governor, considers or rules just for his own personal advantage, but he rules for the benefit of the governed, and to those to whom he ministers. He keeps an eye on this, and considers what is advantageous and suitable to this aim; he both says what he says, and does what he does!'

'But Socrates, the governed do what is for the Governor's advantage, he being the more powerful, and the governed minister to him, promoting his happiness, but by no means their own. You must then consider it most obvious, Socrates, that, on all occasions, the ruler gets the best of it with the ruled getting the worst. First, in co-partnerships, where the one joins in company with the other, you never can find, on the dissolution of that company, that the ruler gives more than the ruled, but less. Then, in civil affairs, where there are taxes to be paid from equal substance, the governed man pays more, the ruler pays less. And when there is anything to be gained, the governed gain nothing, but the gain of the ruler is great!'

'But, for my own part, I must tell you, my good Thrasymachus that I am not persuaded by you, nor do I think that injustice is ever more profitable than justice. I at least believed there was a necessity for us to agree over this, that every government, in so far as it is a government, considers what is best for nothing else but for the governed, and those under its charge, both in political and private government. Is this not self-evident, Thrasymachus, that no true art of government provides what is advantageous for itself, but, as I said long ago, provides and enjoins what is most advantageous for the governed, always, having in view the profit of the inferior, and not that of the more powerful?

'And, for these reasons, friend Thrasymachus, I likewise say now, that no one who is willing to govern, and to undertake to rectify the ills of others, asks a reward for it; because, whoever will perform that art efficiently never acts just for what is best for himself. In ruling, he tries to do what is best for the governed. On this account, it seems, a reward must be given to those who shall be willing to govern, either by money or honour. And if they will not govern justly they should be punished. The just man resembles the wise and the good; and the unjust resembles the evil and the ignorant. The just man has appeared to me to be good and wise, and the unjust to be wicked and depraved.'

Thrasymachus eventually agreed to all these things I had said, but not easily, but looked on with difficulty and sweated prodigiously, it being now the summer season. And I then saw, for the first time, but never before, Thrasymachus blush. After that he acknowledged that true justice was virtue and wisdom, and injustice was vice and ignorance.

'Well,' I said, 'let this remain so, for it was said by you earlier that injustice was more powerful and stronger than justice. But now, I say, since justice is both virtue and wisdom, it will easily, I imagine, appear to be more powerful than injustice. Since injustice is ignorance, of this point of view, now none should be ignorant. Do you imagine that a city, or a camp, or robbers, or thieves, or any other community, such as jointly undertakes to do anything unjustly, is able to effect anything if they injure one another? But what, if they do not injure one another, will they not do better? For injustice somehow, Thrasymachus, brings sedition, and hatred, and fighting among them; but justice leads to harmony and friendship.

'The unjust man, Thrasymachus, shall be an enemy also to the Gods; and the just man, a friend. At no time is injustice more advantageous than justice.' 'Let that be your festal offering, Socrates,' he said, 'hand this truth to Diana at her festival.'

'Thanks to you, truly, Thrasymachus,' said I, 'since I find you have now grown meek, and have ceased to be troublesome. But I have not feasted well; owing to my own fault, and not to yours. But as voracious guests, snatching what is being brought before them, taste it before they have sufficiently enjoyed what went before; so I have realized, that what we first enquired into, what justice actually is, we have left this out, in our hurry to enquire into it, and ask whether it be vice and ignorance, or wisdom and virtue. And with your argument that injustice was more profitable than justice, I could not refrain from coming to this statement from the opposite point of view.'

BOOK 2

THEORY OF JUSTICE

When I had made these observations I imagined that the debate was at an end, but it seems this was only the introduction, for Glauco, as he is on all occasions most courageous, did not approve of Thrasymachus giving up the debate so easily, but said, 'Socrates, do you wish just to seem to have persuaded friend Thrasymachus, or to persuade us in reality that in every respect it is better to be just than unjust. They say, Socrates, that both with Gods and men there is a better life prepared for the unjust man than for the just.'

When Glauco had said these things, I had a wish to say something in reply. But his brother Adimantus then said, 'Socrates, don't imagine that enough has been said on this argument.' 'What further then,' said I, 'that has not yet been spoken, should more be said? Therefore I must go through all the arguments opposed to what Thrasymachus has said further, by which I commend justice and condemn injustice.

'Firstly, parents usually tell and exhort their sons, as do all those who have the care of any children, that it is necessary to be just, not commending justice in itself, but the honours arising from it, and that as long as a man is reputed to be just, he may obtain by this reputation, mag- istracies, the offices of performing marriages, and so forth. But these parents carry this matter of reputation further, for by throwing in the approval of the Gods, they speak of the innumerable blessings they give to just persons. Some even carry the rewards from the Gods still further, for they say that for the offspring of the just, and the faithful, and their children's children, these blessings will stay with them. With these arguments they commend justice. But the unholy and unjust they say, the Gods will bury in Hades, in a kind of slime, and be compelled to carry water in a sieve, and force them, even while alive, to live in infamy!'

'But besides that,' said Adimantus, 'Socrates, consider another kind of reasoning concerning justice and injustice, mentioned both privately and by the poets. For all of them with one accord celebrate temperance and justice as indeed being most excellent, but yet very difficult and laborious to achieve, while intemperance and injustice are indeed very pleasant and easy to attain, by popular opinion, even if considered by law to be abominable. They show them as examples, many books of Musæus and Orpheus, according to which they perform their sacred rites, persuading not only private persons, but States likewise, that there are absolutions and purgations from iniquities by means of sacrifices, sports and pleasures. And this is for the benefit both of the living and of the dead. These they call the Mysteries which absolve us from evils.

'But they assert that dreadful things await those who do not offer sacrifice. All these, and so many things of this kind, friend Socrates, being said of virtue and vice, and their reputation both with men and Gods; what do we imagine the souls of our youth will do, when they hear them, such of them as are generous, and able to talk one with another about all these things, and for all to hear. So with what sort of character and on what sort of road should one best travel through life?

'We should still prefer justice before the greatest injustice, which if we shall attain without any hypocritical appearance of decency, we shall fare well according to our minds, both with reference to the Gods and to men, both alive and dead. By what means, Socrates, shall he incline to honour justice, who has any benefit of fortune, wealth, body or birth, and not laugh when he hears it commended? So that, although a man was even able to show what we have said to be false, and fully understood that justice is better, he will, however, abundantly pardon and not be angry with the unjust. For he knows, that unless, springing from one's own divine nature, one abhors to do injustice, or from acquired knowledge abstains from it, no one of us is willingly just. But either through cowardice, old age, or some other weakness, condemns the doing of injustice when unable to commit it himself. That it is so is plain.

'For the first of these who arrives at power is the first to do injustice. And the reason for all this, is no other than that from where all this discourse proceeded, by you Socrates, saying that among all those of you that call yourselves the commenders of justice, beginning from those ancient heroes of whom any accounts are left to the men of the present time; no one has at any time condemned injustice, nor commended justice, otherwise than by regarding the reputations, honours and rewards arising from them. No one has hitherto sufficiently examined, either in poetry or in prose, either of them in themselves. For it subsists by its own power, in the soul, concealed from both Gods and men that injustice is the greatest of all the evils which the soul has within it, and justice the greatest good.

'For, if it has from the beginning, been said by you to all of us, and you had so persuaded us from our youth, that we should not need to watch over our neighbour because he might do us an injustice. And every man would be the best Guardian over himself, afraid, unless in doing injustice he should dwell with the greatest evil. These things now, Socrates, and probably much more than these, Thrasymachus or some other might say of justice and injustice, inverting their power, as a piece of vulgarity, as I also believe, for my own part.

'But I want to conceal nothing from you, being anxious to hear you speak from the opposite side, and to speak the best as you are able, arguing the contrary way. Do not, therefore, only show us in your reasoning that justice is better than injustice; but in what manner, each of them by itself, affecting the mind, is the one evil, and the other good. And take away all opinions, as Glauco likewise said, for, if you do not take away the false opinions on both sides, and only add the true ones, we will say you do not commend justice, but the appearance of it, nor condemn being unjust, but only the appearance of it.

'Therefore, after you have acknowledged that justice is among the greatest Good, and is most worthwhile to be possessed, from what arises from Her, and much more in themselves, such as better sight, hearing, wisdom, health, and other benefits as are real in their own nature, and not merely in the opinions of others. In the same way commend justice, how, in itself, it profits the owner, and injustice hurts him. So leave it to others to commend rewards and reputations. For I could put up with others in this way, commending justice, and condemning injustice, celebrating and reviling their opinions and rewards, but not from you, unless you desire me to, because you have passed the whole of life considering very little else but this question.

'Show us, then, in your discourse, not only that justice is better than injustice; but in what manner each of them by itself, affecting the owner, is the one good, and the other evil!'

To which I answered, 'Well spoken, Adimantus, your oratorical powers are improving. But I truly cannot give you any further assistance, for I think myself to be unable, and my reason is simply, that you do not accept what I said to Thrasymachus when I honestly believed that I showed that justice was better than injustice. Nor can I think of giving any further arguments, although, I am very much afraid unless it be considered unholy to desert justice when I am present, and when I see it accused, I fail to assist Her, while I still breathe and am able to speak. It may then be best to praise it in such a manner as I can.'

Then Glauco and all the rest entreated me to assist, and not relinquish the discourse, but to search thoroughly though each proposition to explain what it is, and in which way the truth lies, and as to their respective advantage. I then said, 'It seems to me, that the enquiry we are attempting is no trifling matter in the great investigation concerning the real meaning of justice. For, justice in the State is the true work of the Guardians and is one of the greatest importance, and it should require the greatest freedom from other burdensome occupations, and be their all-consuming art and study. And shall it not require a competent genius for this profession? And it should surely be our business, if we are able, to choose who and what kind of men are the most competent for the high office of the Guardianship of our ideal city.

'However, we are not to despair, so long as we have any skill in reasoning left. Do you think that the genius of a generous hunting hound differs in any way from Guardianship, as that found in generous, intelligent youth? Must not each of them be acute in perception, swift to pursue what they sense, and strong, if there is need to conquer what they catch?' 'There is a need,' said Adimantus, 'of all these qualities, and surely he must be brave, if he is to fight well.' 'To be sure,' I said. 'And with reference to his soul he should be spirited. But, it is necessary, that towards their friends they are meek, and fierce towards their enemies, for otherwise they must not wait until others destroy them, which will prevent them doing it themselves.

'What then,' said I, 'shall we do? Where shall we find, at once, the mild and the magnanimous youthful temper? For the mild disposition is somehow opposed to the spirited. Are you, further, of the opinion, that he who is to be our Guardian should, besides being spirited, also be a philosopher? To be a lover of true learning, and to be a philosopher, are identical. May we not then boldly settle it, that in man too, if anyone is to be of a mild disposition towards those of his household and acquaintance, he has the potential to be a philosopher and a lover of learning? So, having granted this proposition, I firmly believe that whoever is to be a good and worthy Guardian for us, of our ideal city, should be a philosopher, and spirited, and swift, and strong in his disposition.

'Let then our Guardian be such a one, but in what manner shall they be educated and instructed? And will the consideration of this be of any assistance to us, in perceiving in what way justice and injustice arise in the city; so that we may not omit any necessary part of the discourse, nor over-consider any matter which is superfluous? What then is the right education? Or, is it difficult to find a better one than that which was found long ago, which is, gymnastics for the body, and harmonic music to soothe the soul?

'Shall we first begin with instructing them in music, rather than in gymnastics?' 'When you say music, you really mean harmonious discourses, do you not?' Adimantus said. 'I do, up to a point, but also real music too. Concerning discourses, there are two kinds, the one true, and the other false, and they must be educated in both, and first in the false. Understand,' said I, 'that we first of all tell children fables and this is part of the music of discourse. For fables, somehow, in what they say in general, are false, yet there is truth hidden in them, and we should accustom children to love fables before their gymnastic exercises. This is what I meant, when I said that children were to begin music before gymnastics.

'And do you not know that the beginning of every work is of the greatest importance, especially to anyone who is young and tender? For then, truly, in the easiest manner, is formed the impressions which one wishes to imprint on every individual. Shall we permit the children to hear any kind of fables composed by just any kind of persons, and to receive, for the most part, into their minds, opinions contrary to those that we judge they ought to have when they are grown up? First of all, we must preside over the fable-makers. And whatever beautiful fables they make must be specially chosen; and what are harmful must be rejected. And we shall persuade the nurses and mothers to tell the children such fables as shall be selected, and to fashion their minds by fables, much more than their bodies by their gymnastics.

'Also, it is not to be said in the hearing of a youth, that he who does wickedness does nothing wrong. Neither should we say that he who in any way punishes his unjust father does the same as the first and the greatest of the Gods. Neither must it be told to them how Gods war with Gods, and plot and fight against one another, for such assertions are not true. At least, those who are to be the Guardians of our city, for us, ought to account it the most shameful thing to hate one another on the slightest grounds. Likewise we should not tell in fables, and embellish them, with the battles of the giants, and the many other various feuds, both of Gods and heroes, with their own kindred and relations. For we are to persuade them that at no time should one citizen hate another, and that it is unholy!

'Such advice should be given to them immediately when they are children, by the older men and women, and those well advanced in life. The poets are also to be obliged to compose in agreement with these ideas, for the young person is not able to judge what is allegory and what is not. For whatever opinions he receives at such an early age, are with difficulty washed away, and are generally immovable in later life. For these reasons, one must affirm, and we should make sure that what they are first to hear, be composed in the most wholesome manner, so encouraging them to virtuous behaviour?

'God is always to be represented such as He is, whether one represents Him in epic, in song, or in tragedy. This must be done. For, isn't God essentially Good, and is He not to be described as such? And nothing which is Good is hurtful, is it? Does that which is not hurtful ever do further hurt? Does that which does not hurt do any further evil? And what does no evil cannot be the cause of any further evil.

'Very well, the Good is beneficial; it is, the cause of welfare. The Good, therefore, is not the cause of all things, but the cause of those things which are in a right state; but is not the cause of those things which are in a wrong state. Neither, then, can God,' I said, 'since He is the Good, and is the cause of all things, as many say; but He is also the cause of a few things to most men. For, of many things He is not the cause, for good things are much fewer than evil things, and none other than God is the cause of our good things, and of evil things, we must not make God the cause, but seek for some other explanation. We must say that God always does what is just and good, and that the wicked are benefited by being chastised.

'But we must not allow a poet to say that they are miserable who are punished, and that it is God who does these things. But if they say that the wicked, being miserable, needed correction, and that, in being punished, they were profited by God, we may permit that assertion. But, to say that God, who is good, is the cause of ill to anyone, this we must by all means oppose, nor allow anyone to say so in this city, if he wishes to have it well regulated.

'Nor must we permit anyone, either young or old, to hear such things told in fable, either in verse or in prose; as they neither conform to sanctity, nor should be told to children, nor are they profitable for us, nor consistent with themselves. This, may be one of the laws and models with reference to the Gods, by which it shall be necessary that those who speak, and who write, shall compose, and say that God is not the cause of all things, but only of the Good.

'Now for this second law. Do you think that God is a magician, and insidiously appears, at different times, in different shapes, sometimes like Himself, and, at other times, changing His appearance into many shapes. Sometimes deceiving us, and making us conceive false opinions of Him? Or, do you believe Him to be simple, and not departing from

His proper form? If anything be changed from its proper form, is there not a necessity that it be changed by itself, or by another? Are not those matters which are in the best state least of all changed and moved by any other thing?

'And as to the soul itself, will not any perturbation from without, even disorder and change the most brave and wise? And surely, somehow, all utensils which are well made, and buildings, and vestments, according to the same reasoning; such as are properly worked, and in a right state, are least changed by time, or other accidents. Everything which is in a good state, made either by nature, or art, or both, should only receive the smallest change from anything else; but God, and everything belonging to divinity are in the best state.

'In this way, God should least of all have many shapes. It is impossible for a God to desire to change Himself. But as He is most beautiful and excellent, continues always, to the utmost of His power, invariably in His own form. Do not let the mothers frighten their children, telling them stories wrongly; that they may not, at one and the same time, blaspheme against the Gods, and render their children dastardly. I am saying, that to cheat the soul concerning realities, and to be so cheated, and to be ignorant, and there to have gained and maintained a deceit, is what every one should least of all choose. And a deceit in the soul is what most people especially hate.

'But this distortion of good and evil, as I was now saying, might most justly be called the true cheat or deceit, and forms ignorance in the soul of the deceived person; since to be cheated in words is a kind of injury to what the soul feels; and an image afterwards arises in the soul of whoever cheats. Is that not so? But this real lie is not only hated by the Gods, but by good men also. And in those fables we were discussing, as we do not know how the truth really stood in ancient times, making what appears to be a lie in modern times. So, by telling the truth as it seems to us, as clearly as possible, we make it useful for our children.

'There is then no occasion at all for God to make a lie. The Divine and Godlike nature is, in all respects, without a lie? God is simple and true, both in word and deed, neither is He changed in Himself, nor does He deceive others; neither by visions, nor by discourse, nor by the sending of signs, when we are awake, nor when we sleep. You agree then that this shall be the second model, by which we are to teach and instruct the poets to compose, concerning the Gods, that they are neither magicians, to change themselves, nor to mislead us by lies, either in word or deed? When anyone says such slanders as these about the Gods, we shall show displeasure. And we shall not allow teachers to make use of such falsehoods in the education of our youth. If our Guardians are to be pious, and Godly men, as far as it is possible for men to be.'

BOOK 3

EDUCATION OF YOUTH

'These arguments,' I said, 'are what should be heard, concerning the Gods, from childhood, by those who are to be taught to honour their Gods and their parents, and who are not to despise friendship with one another. But, what now? If they are to be brave, must not fables be narrated to them, and such other truths as may render them unafraid of death? Or, do you imagine that anyone can ever be brave whilst he has this fear within him? Well, do you think that anyone can avoid the fear of death, while he goes on imagining that there is Hades, and that it is dreadful? We ought, it seems to me, to give orders to those who undertake to recite fables of this kind. And implore them never to teach anything concerning the so-called events in Hades, as they will say neither what is true, nor what is profitable to those who are to be our future Guardians, good citizens, or brave soldiers.

'We shall, also request Homer and the other poets not to be indignant if we erase false sentiments about Hades from their works, not that they are unpoetical, and pleasant to be heard, but, the more exaggerated they are, the less they should be heard by our children; for men and women who ought to be free, should be more afraid of slavery than of death. Furthermore, are not all dreadful and frightful stories about Hades to be rejected? Coeytus, and Styx, those in the infernal regions, and bloodless shades, and such other names, in this form, terrify all who hear them. These may, perhaps, serve some other purpose: but we are afraid for our future Guardians, for by such stories, they may be made more effeminate and softer than they should be.'

'We are truly afraid of that weakness,' said Adimantus. 'Are these names to be removed?' 'They are, and the poets must speak and compose using contrary examples. We shall also remove the complaints and lamentations, wailed by illustrious men. This is necessary, if what we have stated is to be so. Consider then, whether we are correctly taking away these speeches, or not? For, do we not believe that the worthy man will say that to die is not so dreadful, to his companions? Neither will he grieve over death, as if his friend suffered some dreadful calamity. And we say this also, that such a person first of all must be sufficient in himself, for the purpose of living happily, and in a manner to be distinguished from all others he is never scornful.

'It is to him, less dreadful to be deprived of a son, a brother, wealth, or any other such-like possessions. So that he will not grieve, but endure, in the bravest manner, when any such misfortune befalls him. We shall rightly then take away the mourning of famous men, and assign them to the women, so that all those whom we propose to educate for the Guardianship of our State may cease to lament. But much more so, we must entreat them not to make the Gods lament. They must not, therefore, do that, as our reasoning has now convinced us, which we must trust, until someone else persuades us by some better argument.

'And, surely, neither should we be prone to excessive laughter, for, where a man gives himself up to violent laughter, such a disposition commonly leads to a violent attack of apoplexy. And, if anyone represents worthy men as being overcome by laughter, should we allow it, especially if he refers to the Gods.' 'Yes, indeed. This is not to be permitted, according to your reasoning.' 'If you incline,' I said, 'to call it my reasoning alone, that is also not to be admitted. But surely the truth is much to be valued. For, if lately we have reasoned rightly, and if indeed a lie be unprofitable when told about the Gods, but useful to some men, in the way of a medicine, it is plain that such a remedy is to be entrusted only to the physicians, but not to be used by private persons.

'It belongs then to the Governors and Guardians of the city, if to any others, to make such falsifications, with reference either to enemies or citizens, for the good of the city; but none of the rest should venture on such an enterprise. But for a private person to tell a lie to the Governors, we will condemn in the same way. And it's even a greater offence, for the patient to tell a lie to the physician. Or for the man who learns his exercises, not to tell his master the truth, as to the disposition of his mind and body, as it is for a pilot not to tell his captain, the real state of affairs, respecting his ship and sailors, and their condition. And if you find in the city anyone else inventing such lies, you shall punish them, as introducing a practice that's subversive and destructive to the city, as on a ship.

'Also, shall not our youth need the virtue of temperance? And are not such qualities as these, the principal parts of temperance? That they be obedient to their Governors, and that the Governors themselves be temperate in drinking, feasting, and in venereal pleasures. And we shall say, I imagine, that such things as these are well, as Diomed says in Homer, "Sit thou in silence, and obey my speech. The

Greeks marched on in silence, breathing force. Revering their commanders…" and so on.' 'Well spoken. But what about these verses? "Then the drunkard with dog's eyes, and heart of deer" and all lines of this kind, such as these, or any other insolences, which any private person in prose or poetry has been made to say against their Governors. Are they spoken worthily?' 'Most unworthily; for I do not believe that when they are heard, they are fit to promote temperance in youth. And although they may give a pleasure of a different kind, these words do not seem to be appropriate.

'But any instances of self-denial,' said I, 'which are practised by eminent men, these are to be taken note of and heard. For example, we should not commend Achilles, or approve of his being so covetous as to receive presents from Agamemnon, and similarly receive a ransom to give up the dead body of Hector, but not incline to do it otherwise. I am unwilling, for Homer's sake, to say it, that it is unlawful that these lines which are spoken against Achilles, or that they should be believed, when said by others, such as the dragging of Hector around the sepulchre of Patroclus, and the slaughtering of the captives at his funeral pile. That these things are true, we will not say, nor will we allow our people to be persuaded that Achilles, the son of a Goddess, and of Peleus, the most temperate of men, and third from Zeus, educated by the wise Chiron, was full of such disorder as to have within him two distempers opposite to one another, that is, the illiberal and the covetous disposition, as well as a contempt both for Gods and men.

'Neither,' I said, 'let us be persuaded in favour of these rumours, or allow any to say that Theseus the son of Poseidon, and Pirithous the son of Zeus, were impelled to perpetrate dire rapines. Or that any son of another deity, or any hero, would dare to do horrible and impious deeds, such as the lies that some poets ascribe to them. But let us compel the poets either to say that these are not the actions of these persons, or that these persons are not the children of the Gods, but not to say both! Neither let us not permit them to attempt to persuade our youth that the Gods created evil, and that heroes are in no respect better than men. For, as we said formerly, these calumnies are neither holy nor true, for we have elsewhere shown that it is impossible that evil should proceed from the Gods.

'For these slanders are truly hurtful, to the hearers, at least. For every one will pardon his own depravity, when he is persuaded that even the near relations of the Gods commit, and have done such things of the same kind, even those that are near to Zeus. On which account all such fables must be suppressed, as they could create in our youth a powerful tendency to wickedness. What other types of discourse, have we still remaining, now that we are deciding what should be spoken, and what should not? We have already mentioned in what manner we should speak concerning the Gods, and similarly of demons and heroes, and of all that relates to Hades.

'Shouldn't we also decide on what yet remains to be taught concerning men? But it is impossible for us to regulate this at present, because, I think, we would say that the poets and chroniclers speak mistakenly concerning the great affairs of men, such as: "That many men are unjust, and, notwithstanding this, are happy"; and "That many of the just are miserable"; and "That it is profitable for one to do unjustly, when he is concealed"; and "That justice is a gain to others, but a loss to the just man himself". These, and innumerable other falsehoods, we will forbid them to say, and instead encourage them to compose in fable, the opposite of these verses.

'If you acknowledge that what I say is right, shall I not say that you have acknowledged all along what we seek? Shall we also say that such discourses are to be spoken about mankind, only after we have discovered what justice truly is, and how, by its very nature, it is profitable for the just man to be just? Concerning these discourses, then, let this be sufficient. We must now consider, as I believe, the style of discourse. Then we shall have completely considered both what is to be spoken, and the manner of how it is to be spoken.' Here Adimantus said, 'But I do not understand what you say.' I replied, 'It is necessary that you should, and perhaps you should rather understand it in this way. Is not everything spoken by mythologists, or poets, a narrative of the past, present, or future? And don't they execute it, either by simple narration, or by acting, or by both?' 'This too, but I want to understand more clearly.'

'I seem,' I said, 'to be a ridiculous and rather obscure instructor, in such a matter as this, for it seems, both the mythologist and the poets perform the narrative by means of performance, rhapsodizing or declaiming. But if the poet was true to himself, his whole action and narrative could be without acting. And you may say that you do not again understand how this should be. I shall tell you. If Homer, after relating how Chryses came with his daughter's ransom beseeching the Greeks, but chiefly the kings, had spoken afterwards, not as Chryses, but still as Homer, you know it would not have been imitation, but simple narration. And it would have been somehow like this, I shall speak without metre, for I am no poet.

'"The priest came and prayed, that the Gods might grant

[28]

they should take Troy, and return safe; and begged them to restore to him his daughter, accepting the presents, and revering their God." When he'd said this, all the rest showed respect and consented, but Agamemnon was enraged, ordering him to leave instantly, and not to return again, in case his sceptre and the garlands of his God should not be of any help, and told him that before he would restore his daughter she should grow old with him in Argos, and ordered him to be gone, and not to irritate him, that he might return home in safety. The old man upon hearing that injunction, was afraid, and went away in silence. And when he left the camp he made many supplications to Apollo, repeating the names of the God, and reminding him and beseeching him, that if ever he had made any acceptable donation for the building of temples, or the offering of sacrifices, for the sake of these, to avenge his honour against the Greeks with his arrows.

'So, I say, my friend, the narration should be simple, without excessive exaggerated elaboration. Understand that this can happen, when one removes the poet's verses between the actual speeches, and leaves the simple narration alone.' 'This,' Adimantus said, 'I also understand, that this takes place especially respecting the tragedies.' 'You understand perfectly well,' I said, 'and I think that now I shall make it perfectly plain to you what I could not do before, that in poetry, and likewise in mythology, one kind of verse is composed with excessive exaggerated elaboration, such as you say, with tragedy. I think the same could also be said of comedy. There is another kind of narration by the poet himself, and you will find this kind especially in the Dithyrambics. And there's another kind again in epic poetry, and in many other cases, if you follow me?

[29]

'And remember too, before we were saying that we had already discussed what should be spoken; now it remains to be considered in what manner the verses are to be recited. This is what I was saying, that it was necessary we agreed whether we shall allow the poets to declaim narrative to us in the style of exaggerated elaboration.' 'I imagine,' he said, 'that you wish us to consider whether we should accept tragedy and comedy into our city, or not?' 'Perhaps,' I replied, 'and something else also, for I do not yet know, but wherever our reasoning takes us, as in sailing when a gale bears upon us, there we must go.

'Consider this too, Adimantus, whether our Guardians ought to practise poetic elaboration, and be subject to it, or not? Or does it follow from what we have said before, namely that each one may perform one skill well, but not many. Or, if he will try to grasp at many arts, he shall fail in all, so as to be remarkable in none. And is not the reasoning the same concerning elaboration? That one man is not so able to elaborate on many topics as well as one. Hardly is he able to perform any one of the more eminent employments, such as Governor or Guardian, and at the same time elaborate on many subjects, hear or read elaboration. Since the same persons are not able to perform successful elaborations of two different kinds, which seem to resemble each other. For instance, they cannot succeed both in comedy and tragedy, and you lately called these two, elaborations?' 'I did, and Socrates, you speak truly, that the same persons cannot succeed in both of them.'

'True,' I said, 'and if therefore we are to hold to our first reasonings, that our Guardians, uninfluenced or unoccupied by any poetic elaboration whatsoever, would then be the most accurate preservers of the liberty of the city, and to care for nothing other than that which has some reference to this duty. But, if they shall be subject to poetic elaboration at all, it should be from their childhood, when such verses correspond with brave, temperate, holy, free men, and all such heroes as these. But not to desire to represent illiberal or base men, for by imitating bad men, they will come to be really like them. Or have you not observed, that imitations, mimicry or poetic elaborations, made from earliest youth, if they are continued onwards into manhood, become fixed into their manners and natural disposition, with reference to their bodies, voices, and their intellectual powers?

'We shall surely not allow that,' said I, 'those we choose to take care of our city must be good men, and not imitate a woman, either young or old, reviling her husband, or quarrelling with the Gods, or speaking boastingly when she imagines herself to be happy, or to parody her in her misfortunes, sorrows, and lamentations, when sick, in love, or in childbirth. We should not permit this. And poets should not be allowed to imitate men or maid-servants when performing acts that belong to servants. Nor to imitate depraved men, such as are dastardly, and act in the opposite way to what we have been mentioning, such as reviling and railing at one another, and gossiping about abominable lewd acts, when either drunk or sober.

'Furthermore, for that matter, talking loosely, expressing other offensive sentiments, such as persons of this class are guilty of, either in words or deeds, with respect to themselves or to one another. Neither must they ever accustom themselves to resemble madmen, in words or actions. The mad and wicked are to be recognized, both the men and the women, but none of their actions are to be performed or imitated!' 'True,' he said, 'but are they allowed to imitate those who work in brass, or any other handicrafts, or those employed in rowing galleys, or those that command them, or anything else regarding these employments?' 'How can they,' I said, 'as they are not to be allowed to give time to any of these matters?' Then he said, 'How shall they imitate horses neighing, bulls bellowing, rivers murmuring, seas roaring, or thunder clapping, and all such like things?' 'We have forbidden them,' I said, 'to sound as if mad, or to resemble madmen!'

'If I understand what you say,' he replied, 'there is a certain kind of speech, and of narration, in which he who is truly a good and worthy man expresses himself, when it is necessary for him to say anything, and another kind unlike this man, who has been born and educated in an opposite way; but what kind of men are these?' 'It seems to me,' I said, 'that the worthy man, when he recites his narrative of any speech or action of a good man, will willingly tell it as if he were himself that man, and will not be ashamed of such an imitation, most especially choosing to do so when he imitates a good man acting prudently and without error. But less willingly and less fully when the man is weakened through disease, or by passion, intoxication, or any other misfortune. But when he comes to think anything unworthy of himself, he should not regard himself as one who is worse, unless for a short time, when it may produce some good. But he will be ashamed, as he is unpractised in the imitation of such characters as these, and similarly he should not degrade himself and recite from examples of baser characters, affecting his intellectual faculty, and doing it only for amusement.

'He will not make use of such a narrative as we lately mentioned, with reference to the compositions of Homer, but his compositions may participate with poetic elaborations in some other narrative, but a small part of it will be imitation, and the greater part will be plain narrative. And, on the other hand, will not the man who is not such a model, be the more depraved, for he will be ready to rehearse anything whatsoever; and not think anything unworthy of himself? And he will undertake to imitate everything in earnest, and likewise in the presence of many. And such noises as we have just mentioned like thunderings, howling of winds, pattering of hail-stones, axles, wheels, trumpets, pipes, whistles, and all manner of instruments; as well as the voices of dogs, sheep, and birds. And furthermore the whole expression of all these effects shall be by imitation in voice and gesture, and only a small part of it narration. That must happen of necessity and these I call the two kinds of diction.

'But haven't these only small variations? And if the orator lends harmony and measure to the diction, when he speaks with propriety, the discourse is always after one and the same style, and in one harmony, for the variations are small, and in a metre which is somewhat similar. But what as to other kinds of diction? Don't they require the contrary style, allowing all types of harmony, all types of measures, if what is to be said is to be naturally expressed, as it has all kinds of variations? Do not now all the poets, and such as speak in any kind of diction, make use of either one or other of these modes of speech, or of one compounded of both?

'What then shall we do?' I said. 'Should we admit into our ideal city all these modes of diction, one of the unmixed, and one of the compounded?' 'In my opinion,' he replied, 'that uncompounded one prevails, which is imitative of what is most worthy.' 'But surely, Adimantus, the mixed mode is pleasant, at least. And the opposite of what you choose is only the most pleasant to children, pedagogues, and the crowd. But you will not, probably, think it suitable for our Government, because with us, no man is to attend to two or more methodologies at once, but to be quite simple, as everyone usually does only one thing well. Shall we not find that in such an ideal city, a shoemaker is only a shoemaker, and not a pilot along with shoemaking, and that the husbandman is only a husbandman, and not a judge along with husbandry, and the soldier is a soldier, and not a money-maker besides, and all others in the same way?

'And it would seem, that if a man, who, through his wisdom, was able to become proficient at everything, and to imitate everything, and should come into our city, and should wish to show us his poems, we should revere him as a worthy, admirable, and pleasant person, but we should also tell him, that no such poet is to stay with us, and we should send him to some other city, pouring oil on his head, and crowning him with wool. For we prefer a more austere poet, and mythologist, to our advantage, who may recite to us in the finest diction in the most worthy manner: and may say whatever he says, according to those models which we have established by law, when we undertook the education of our soldiers.

'It appears,' I said, 'my dear friend, that we have now thoroughly discussed what I call the fine music of harmonious discourse in respect of recitation, oratory and fable; for we have said what is to be spoken, and in what style. Does it not yet remain that we should speak about the formal composition of song, and of melodies? May not anyone discover what we think in these matters, and of what kind of form these should be, if we are to be consistent with what has been discussed?'

Here Glauco, laughing, said, 'But I seem, Socrates, to be a stranger to all these questions, for I am not able, at present, to understand what we should say or not.' I said, 'I suspect, however, that you are fully able to say that in the first place, melody, which expresses the human soul in music, is composed of three things: sentiment, harmony, and rhythm. And that the part of music which consists of sentiment, differs in no way from that sentiment which is not sung, in so far as it should be performed on the same models, as we have already discussed, and in precisely the same way. And surely, the harmony and rhythm ought to correspond to that same sentiment.

'But we observed there should never be an occasion in our city for wailing, moaning and lamentation in poetic and musical compositions. Which then are the querulous harmonies? Tell me, for you are a musician.' 'The mixed Lydian,' he replied, 'and the sharp Lydian, and some more of this kind.' 'Are not these,' said I, 'to be rejected? For they are unprofitable even to women, such as are worthy, and much more to men. Now, intoxication is also most unbecoming to our Guardians, along with effeminacy and idleness. Which then are the effeminate and convivial harmonies?' 'The Ionic,' he replied, 'and the Lydian; which are called relaxing.' 'Can you make any use of these, my friend, for military men?' 'By no means,' he replied, 'but you still have the Doric, and the Phrygian.'

'I do not know,' I said, 'these harmonies, but let us leave that harmony, which may, in a becoming manner, imitate the voice and accents of a truly brave man, going into a military action, and every rough adventure, fighting his way in a determined and persevering manner. When he fails to succeed, he becomes wounded, or dies, or falls into some other distress. And similarly, we welcome that kind of harmony, which is best suited to what is peaceable; where there is no violence, and everything is voluntary. When a man either persuades or beseeches anyone, about any need, either God by prayer, or man by instruction and admonition. And, also where one submits himself to another, who beseeches, instructs, and persuades, and in all these degrees, accepts according to his teacher's wishes, and does not behave haughtily, humbling himself soberly and moderately, fully content with whatever may happen.

'Leave then these two harmonies, the vehement and the voluntary, which, in the best possible manner, imitate the voice of the unfortunate and of the fortunate, the moderate and the brave. We shall not have any need for a great many strings, nor of the all-modulating style in our songs and melodies. We shall not employ such workmen as make harps and spinets, and all those instruments which consist of many strings, and produce a variety of harmonies. Well, will you admit into your city such workmen as make pipes, or are pipers? For, are not the instruments which consist of the greatest number of strings, and those that produce all kinds of harmony, imitations of the pipe? There's still left the lyre and the harp, as useful for our city, and there might likewise be some kind of a reed for shepherds in the fields. We shall do nothing untoward, if we prefer Apollo, and Apollo's instruments, to Marsyas, and the instruments of that eminent musician. And, we have, without realizing it, cleansed our city, which we said was becoming over luxurious.

'Come,' I said, 'let us clean up what remains concerning rhythm, for that mode should be the most suitable for our harmonies, so that our citizens do not pursue such rhythms which are diversified, and have a variety of cadences. But let us consider what the rhythms are for a decent, manly life, and, while they observe these, make the foot and the melody subservient to sentiments of that kind, and not sentiments which are subservient to the foot and the melody. But what these rhythms are, it is your business to tell us, as you have done with the harmonies.'

'By Zeus,' he replied, 'I cannot tell. There are three divisions from which the notes are composed, as there are four in the sounds from which flows the whole of harmony, as I have observed. But which are the imitations of one kind of life, and which of another, I am unable to tell.' 'So these things,' I said, 'we must consider with Damon's assistance, what notes are suitable to illiberality and insolence, to madness or other ill dispositions; and what notes are proper for their opposites. For, I remember, but not distinctly, having heard him speak of a certain warlike rhythm, composite, with a dactylic, and a heroic measure, used in arranging it. I do not know exactly how, making the rise and fall equal, passing into short and long, and he called one, as I imagine, Iambus, and another Trochæus. He gave them, besides, the longs and shorts, and in some of these, I believe, he blamed and commended the measure of the foot, no less than the numbers themselves, or the compound of both. But I cannot speak about these things, because, as I said, they are to be put to Damon. To speak distinctly, indeed, on these matters, would require a long discourse.

Then I said, 'But can you determine that the propriety or impropriety corresponds to the good or ill rhythm?' 'Yes, of course,' said Glauco. 'But with respect to the good or ill rhythm, the one corresponds to harmonious expression, conforming itself to it, and the other to the opposite. And, in the same way as to the discordant, since the rhythm and harmony are subservient to the sentiment, as we have just now said, and not the sentiment to them.

'But what,' I said 'as to their manner of expression; and to the sentiment itself; must it not correspond to the temperament of the soul? And all other notes must correspond to that expression, so that the beauty of expression, the fine consonance, and the propriety, and the excellence of numbers, are subservient to a good disposition. And not to that stupidity, which in complaisant language we call good temper; but a mind, truly adorned with excellent and beautiful manners. Must not these virtues always be pursued by the youth, if they are to mind their studies?

'But painting, too, is somehow full of these modulations, and so is every other good workmanship. Weaving is full of these subtleties, so is sculpture and architecture, along with all workmanship, making every kind of vessel; as is, moreover, the nature of our bodies, for in all these there is propriety, and impropriety. The impropriety, discord, and dissonance, are the sisters of ill expression, and depraved manners, while their opposites are the sisters of sober and worthy manners. Are we, then, to give instructions to the poets alone, and oblige them to work into their compositions the image of worthy manners, or not to compose at all with us? Or are we to enjoin all other workmen similarly, and restrain their ill, undisciplined, illiberal, indecent manners, so that they do not exhibit it either in their representations of animals, buildings, or in any other workmanship? And that he who is not able to do this be disallowed from working with us? In case our Guardians, being educated in the centre of bad representations, feed like sheep in a sick pasture, each day plucking and munching very much indifferent food. Little by little, this unhealthy diet contacts imperceptibly, some wickedness in their souls.

'But we must look for such workmen as are able, by the help of a good natural disposition, to investigate the nature of the beautiful and the Good, so that our fine youth, living as it were in a healthy place, may profit on all sides. Because from beautiful works something will be conveyed to the sight and hearing, as a pleasant breeze wafts health from amenable places, gently leading them on directly from childhood, to the virtues of good friendship and harmony, with sound reasoning encouraged.

'For these reasons therefore, Glauco, is not education in music of the greatest importance, because rhythm and harmony enter strongly into the inward part of the soul, and most powerfully affect it, introducing at the same time decorum, and making one refined and decent, if he is well educated, and the opposite happens if he is not? And, moreover, because the man here, who has been well educated as he should be, sees in the quickest manner possible what workmanship is defective, and what execution is unworthy. Then being disgusted by such decadence, he will praise what is beautiful, rejoicing in it, receiving it into his soul, be nourished by it, and become a worthy and good citizen. But whatever is base, he will quite properly despise and hate whilst he is still young, and before he is able to be capable of sound reason. And when that reason dawns, such a one who has been so well educated will embrace it, recognizing it perfectly well, from its intimate familiarity with himself.

'The same is true with reference to letters,' I said, 'for we are well instructed when we are familiar with the grammar, and when we do not despise the rules as being unnecessary to be observed. Then, by all means we endeavour to understand them thoroughly, as it is impossible for us to be literary men until we can do this well! It is indeed as I say, that we shall never become musicians, neither we ourselves, nor those Guardians we are to educate, before we understand the forms of temperance, fortitude, liberality, munificence, and the other sister virtues. And, on the other hand, the opposites of these, which are everywhere to be met with, observe them wherever they are, together with the virtues themselves, and not despise them, but accept that they belong to the same noble arts and studies.

'Must not,' I said, 'the person who shall contain in his soul the beauties of manners and virtue, and in his appearance be seemly, as a model of the finest anyone is able to be? For who and what are most beautiful are most admired. He who is musical would surely love those musicians who are most eminent in this way; but if anyone is inharmonious or discordant in his disposition he could not love him.' 'He shall not,' he replied, 'if the person is any way defective in his soul. For if indeed it were only in his body, he could bear with it, so as still to be willing to associate with him.' 'I understand,' I said, 'that your best friends are, or have been, of this type, and I agree to you keeping such companionship. But tell me this; is there any correspondence between temperance and excessive pleasure?' 'How can there be?' he said. 'For much excessive pleasure causes a privation of intellect as well as grief.' 'But has excess of pleasure a correspondence with any other virtue?' 'By no means!' 'Well, has it any relationship with insolence and intemperance? In my opinion the right disposition is of such a nature as to love the beautiful, in a temperate and disciplined manner.

'Nothing then which is insane, or allied to intemperance, can be an approach to true love. Neither must excessive pleasure approach it, nor must the lover, and the person he loves, have a relationship with it, when they love and are beloved in a right manner. So it seems you will establish by law in our city, which is one day, hopefully, to be established, that the lover is to love, to converse, and associate with the object of his love, as with his son or daughter, for the sake of virtue. And as to everything else besides, that everyone who so converses with him, and whose love he solicits, should never appear to associate with anything beyond what we have now mentioned; otherwise he shall undergo the reproach of being discordant, and unacquainted with the beautiful.

'Does,' I said, 'this discourse concerning music, seem to you now to be completed? For it has terminated where it ought to terminate, as the affairs of such harmony ought somehow to terminate in the love of the beautiful. Now, after music, our youth are to be educated in gymnastics. Then it is surely necessary that likewise they be correctly disciplined, from their infancy through the whole of their life. For in this matter, I think that a good soul, by its virtuous nature, renders the body, the best that is possible.

'If when we have sufficiently cultivated our mind, we should then commit it to the accurate management of bodily concerns? We say that they are to abstain from intoxication, for it is forbidden for a Guardian to be intoxicated and not to know where he is. But what about their meals? For these men are wrestlers in the noblest combat of the soul are they not? Would not the diet of wrestlers be proper for men such as these?' 'Probably.' 'But perhaps not,' I said, 'for it's of a drowsy kind, and doubtful for good health. Don't you observe that these gladiators sleep out their life? And, if they depart just a little from their regular diet, such wrestlers become extremely ill. But some more elegant diet is necessary for our military wrestlers with the soul; who, like good watch dogs, should be wakeful, to see, and hear most acutely; and, in their spiritual expeditions, to endure many different changes in water and food, heat and cold, so that they may never suffer from bad health.

'Are not then the best gymnastics a kind of sister to the refined, harmonious music, which we earlier defined?' 'How do you mean?' 'That the gymnastic regime is to be simple and moderate, and of that kind most especially which applies to battle. Even from Homer,' said I, 'one may learn about these matters for, you know, in their warlike expeditions, at the entertainments of their heroes, they are never feasted with fishes, and that even while they were by the sea at the Hellespont, they were never served with boiled flesh, but only with roasted; and that which soldiers can most easily procure. In short, one can everywhere make use of fire, and carry utensils about.

'Neither does Homer, as I have read, anywhere make any mention of spicy seasonings, and this is what the other wrestlers understand, that the body which is to be in good trim, must abstain from hot spices.' 'They understand correctly,' he said, 'and they abstain.' 'You do not, my friend, approve of the Syracusan table, and the Sicilian variety of meats, since this other diet seems to you to be right? You will likewise disapprove of a Corinthian girl as a mistress, for they are supposed not to have very good bodily habits. And similarly, those delicacies of Attic confections.

'For all feeding and dieting of this kind, we should compare it to the refined melody and song produced in the style of many harmonious modulations, and rhythms. Is that not a just comparison? And does not diversity in such a case create intemperance and disease? But dietary simplicity, as with harmonious music, creates temperance in the soul, and, as with gymnastics, health to the body.

'So when intemperance and diseases multiply in the city, don't we need to have many halls of justice and medicine opened? And will not the art of justice and of medicine be in demand, when many free persons earnestly apply for them? But can you deduce any greater example of an ill and base education in a city than that there should be a great need for physicians and magistrates, not only for those working in low handicrafts, but for those who boast of having been educated in a liberal manner? And doesn't it seem to be shallow, and a great sign of want of education, to be obliged to suffer from justice pronounced on us by others, as our masters and judges, and to have no sense of it in ourselves? And don't you think this to be more shallow still, when one not only spends a great part of one's life in courts of justice, as defendant or plaintiff, but, also from ignorance of the beautiful and the Good.

'Imagine the man or woman that becomes renowned for being dexterous in committing injustice, and able to twist through all kinds of windings, and using every kind of subterfuge, tries to escape and evade justice, and all this for the sake of small contemptible gains. All because he is ignorant about how much better it is to regulate his life, so as not to stand in front of a sleepy judge? And to stand in need of medicinal skill,' I said, 'it is not always on account of wounds, or some incidental epidemic, but through sloth, and such a diet as we mentioned, being filled with rheums and wind, like quagmires, obliging the skilful sons of Asclepius to invent new names for diseases, such as dropsy and catarrh. Don't you think this is abominable?

'Such', I said, 'was never the case in the days of Asclepius, and I deduce from this that when Eurypylus was wounded at Troy, and was being given some Pramnian wine to drink with much flour in it, and the addition of cheese, all which seem to be feverish, the sons of Asclepius did not blame the woman who served it, nor admonish Patroclus, who had prescribed the cure.' 'Surely that medicine,' he said, 'is absurd for one in such a case.' 'No,' said I, 'if you consider that, as they tell us, the descendants of Asclepius did not, before the days of the Herodiens, practise this method of cure now in use, which puts the patient on a special diet.

'But Heroditus being a trainer of youth, and at the same time infirm in his health, mixed gymnastics and medicine together, and felt himself to be most uneasy in the first place, and afterwards too.' 'After what manner?' he said. 'In procuring for himself,' I said, 'a lingering death. For while he was constantly attentive to his disease, which was mortal, he was not able, I imagine, to cure himself through neglecting everything else. Besides, he was still using medicines like this, and he passed his life in the greatest uneasiness if he departed in the least from his accustomed diet. Yet, through his wisdom, struggling long with death, he arrived at a ripe old age. Such becomes one who did not understand that it was not from ignorance or inexperience of this method of cure that Asclepius did not leave it to his descendants, but because he knew that, in all well regulated States, there was some certain work for everyone in the city, which was necessary to be done, and that no one was to be allowed to have the leisure of being sick through the whole of his life, and to be occupied only in taking medicines.

'This we may often observe in the case of labouring people, but we do not observe it in the case of the well-off, and such as are counted happy. A smith, when he falls ill, thinks it fit to take from the physician some medicine, to throw off his disease, or purge it. Or even by means of caustic plasters or amputation to be freed from the trouble. But if anyone prescribes for him a long regimen, putting weights on his head, and other such practices, he quickly tells him that he hasn't the leisure to lie sick, nor does it benefit him to live in this manner, attentive to his trouble, and negligent of his proper work. So, bidding such a physician farewell, he returns to his ordinary diet. And, if he recovers his health, he continues to manage his own affairs, but if his body is unable to bear the disease, he dies, and is freed from trouble.'

'It seems proper,' he said, 'for such a patient to use the medicinal art in this manner.' 'Is it not,' I said, 'because he had a certain business, which if he did not perform well, it was not to his advantage to live? But the rich man, as we say, has no such work allotted him, from which if he is obliged to refrain, life is not worth living. For you do not pay attention to what Phocylides says, that one ought, as soon as there is enough to live on, to practise virtue. Let us by no means,' I said, 'disagree with him in this opinion, but let us inform ourselves that how to practise virtue should be the business of the rich, and that life is not worth living if he does not attempt this most worth task. And consider whether this excessive attention to one's disease is indeed a hindrance of the mind's application to masonry and other skills. But, with respect to the exhortation of Phocylides, it is not a hindrance.' 'Yes, by Zeus,' he said, 'it is, and in the greatest degree, whenever this excessive care of the body goes beyond the bounds of sound gymnastics.'

'Nor does it agree with attention to one's private affairs, or military expeditions, or sedentary magistracies in the city. But what is of the greatest importance is that hypochondria is ill fitted for any sort of learning, and enquiry, and study of one's self, while one is perpetually dreading certain pains and headaches, and blaming philosophy for causing them; so that where there is no attention to health, it is a great obstacle to the practice of virtue and self-improvement. For it makes us always imagine that we are ill, and always complaining about the body. And shall we not say that Asclepius understood these things, when for persons with a healthy constitution, and those whom are used to wholesome habits, but were nevertheless afflicted by some particular disease, then for such a constitution he prescribed medicine, repelling their diseases by drugs and incisions, while he encouraged them to observe their accustomed manner of life, so that the public might not suffer any damage?

'But he did not attempt, by prescribing a nourishing diet, to cure such constitutions as were wholly diseased, as it would only prolong a long and miserable life for the man himself. And any descendants who might spring from him would probably be of the same kind. For he did not think the man ought to be cured who could not live healthily in the normal way, as he would be neither profitable to himself nor to his family or the State.' 'You make Asclepius,' said he, 'into a politician.' 'It is plain,' I said, 'that he was so; and do you not see that his sons at Troy excelled in war, and likewise practised medicine in the way I mentioned?

'Or don't you remember, that when Menelaus was wounded by Pandarus, they *"washed off the blood, and softening drugs were applied"*? But, as to what was necessary for him to eat or drink afterwards, they prescribed for him no more than for Eurypylus, believing external applications were sufficient to heal men, who, before they were wounded, were healthy and moderate in their living, whatever mixtures they happened to have drunk at the time. But they judged that to have a diseased constitution, and to live an intemperate life was neither profitable to the men themselves nor to others, and that their art ought not to be employed on those incurables, nor to minister to them, not even though they were richer than Midas!

'It is proper, though in opposition to us, the writers of tragedy, such as Pindar, call Asclepius a son of Apollo, and say that he was bribed by gold to undertake the cure of a rich man, who was already in a deadly state, for which misdeed he was even struck with a thunderbolt. But we are in agreement with what has formerly been said, and will not believe them in these accusations. We will affirm that if he was a son of the God, he was not inclined to be bribed by filthy lucre; or if he was inclined to be bribed, he was not a son of the God.' 'These revelations,' he said, 'are mostly correct. But what do you say, Socrates, as about this? Isn't it necessary to provide good physicians for the welfare of the state? And must not these, be those who have been conversant with a great number of healthy and sick people? And these men should be the best physicians, who have been conversant with all kinds of dispositions?'

I said, 'Yes, but do you know whom I think to be such good men?' 'If you tell me,' he replied, 'I shall endeavour to think likewise.' I replied, 'But you are enquiring into one question about two different matters.' 'How?' he said. 'Physicians,' I replied, 'would become most expert if, beginning from their infancy, they would, when learning the art, be conversant with the greatest number of patients, and these the most sickly; and work with all manner of diseases, even if by their natural constitution they were not necessarily altogether healthy themselves. For it is not by the body, I believe, that they cure the body, or else their own bodies would at no time be ill, but they cure the body by the soul. Which, while if it is ill, isn't capable of performing any cure well.

'But the Judge, my friend, governs the soul by the soul, which, if from his childhood, he has been educated with depraved souls and has been conversant with them, and has himself committed all manner of evils; he is not able to diagnose accurately, as happens in the diseases of the body. But he must in his youth be unpolluted by evil manners, if he means to be good in himself, and be fit to judge soundly about what is justice. Hence the virtuous in their youth appear to be clear minded, and are not easily deceived by the unjust, as they have not within themselves dispositions similar to those of the wicked.'

'But,' he said, 'they often suffer extremely.' 'For which reason,' I said, 'the good judge is not to be a young man, but an elderly man, who's wise in learning about wickedness; what it is, and seeing it not as a kindred possession residing in his own soul, but as a foreign one in the souls of others, which he has for a long time studied, and has understood what sort of an evil it is, by the help of science rather than by his own experience.' 'Such a one,' said he, 'is likely to be the noblest and best judge.' 'And a good one too,' I said, 'which is what is required. For he who has a good soul is truly Good.

'But the other notable, yet suspicious man, who has committed much iniquity himself, when indeed he talks with those like him, being thought to be subtle and wise by others, and appearing to be a worthy man, is extremely cautious, having an eye to those tendencies which he has in himself. Yet, when he approaches the Good, and the more elderly, he appears foolish, suspicious, and out of season, and ignorant of the integrity of good manners, as having within himself, no examples of such kind. But, however, being more frequently conversant with the wicked than with the wise, he deceives himself and others that he is wise, rather than ignorant. We must not, therefore,' said I, 'look for such a one to be a wise and good judge, but only the truly good man. For vice can never know virtue. But virtue, when the temperament has been instructed by experience, shall attain to the knowledge of both its own self and depravity. This man or woman, and not the wicked ones, are the wise.

'Will you then establish in the city such a method of medicine as we have mentioned, along with such a method of judicature as shall carefully preserve for you, those of your citizens who are naturally well disposed both in mind and in body? And, with respect to those who are otherwise, such as are so unwell in their bodies that they shall be permitted to die. But such as are of an evil nature, and incurable with respect to their soul, these they shall permit to die? And it is clear, that our youth will be afraid of needing this judiciary, whilst they are employed listening with attention to that harmonious music, which we know generates temperance. And, according to the very same steps of reasoning, the musician who is willing to pursue gymnastics will choose to perform, so as not to require any medicine unless there is a real necessity. And he will perform his exercises, and his labours, rather looking to the spirited part of his nature, than looking to physical strength, and not as the other wrestlers, who eat and drink and engage in labours for the sake of bodily domination.

'Why then,' said I, 'Glauco, do they who propose to teach music and gymnastics, teach only to cure the body, but not to enliven the soul. Don't you see how these affect their minds, for example those who have all their life been conversant with gymnastics, but have never applied themselves to harmonious music?' 'What,' he said 'are you talking about?' 'Rudeness,' I said, 'and rigidity, as opposed to gentleness and mildness.' 'I know,' said he, 'that those who apply themselves immoderately to gymnastics, become much ruder than is normal; and those again who attend to music alone, are more effeminate than it is becoming for them to be.' 'And surely,' I said, 'this rudeness, may come from the spirited part of nature, but when rightly disciplined, may become bravery, but, when carried further is likely to be both rigid and troublesome

'Well, doesn't the philosophic temper control the mind? But we say that our Guardians ought to have both these dispositions. Ought not these two steeds be harnessed one to another? And the soul in which they are reined, become both temperate and brave. But the soul in which they are not amenable is cowardly and savage. And when one gives himself up to be soothed with the charms of music, and lets its enchanting chords pour into his soul through his ears, as through a conduit, these we call the soft effeminate, and plaintive harmonies, and they may spend their whole life chanting and being ravished by such melodies. But, such a one, at the earliest opportunity, if he has anything spirited in him, melts it like iron, and, from being useless and hard, renders it profitable. But when still persisting, if he does not desist, but continues to enchant his soul, after this, it melts and dissolves in him, until it attenuates his spirit, and cuts out, as it were, the nerves of his soul, and turns him into an effeminate warrior.

'Again, if one labours too much in gymnastics, and feasts extremely well, but does not apply oneself to music and philosophy; shall he not, in the first place, having formed his body in a good condition, be filled with spirit and courage, and become braver than he was before? But what, when he does nothing else, and does not participate in any activity which is musical, as if there wasn't any love of learning in his soul, as he neither studies, nor bears a part in any enquiry nor in reasoning, mustn't he become lame, deaf, and blind; as his perceptions are neither awakened, nor nourished, nor refined? Such a one becomes, as I imagine, an ignoramus, and unmusical, and by no means can he be persuaded to pursue any self-advancement by reasoning. Instead he is carried forward to everything by force and savagery, like a wild beast, and so lives in ignorance and barbarism, out of kilter, and unpolished.

'Regarding these two temperaments, I would say that some God has appeared, and has given men two arts, those of music and gymnastics, in reference to the spirited and philosophic temperament, that those two might be adapted to one another; being stretched and slackened as far as it is fit. Whoever shall in the most effective manner combine gymnastics with music, and contain in these two, a balanced measure in his soul, we shall properly call the more completely musical, and the most harmonious. He is far more so than the man who adjusts to one another of the musical strings. Shall we not then, Glauco, always have need of such a Governor to rule our state, if our government is to be preserved? These may be our models of education and discipline. For why should one search the dances, the hunting of wild beasts, with dogs and nets, the wrestlings and horse-races to find such persons? It is manifestly certain that these qualities may naturally follow in due course, and it is not a difficult matter to find them.'

He then replied, 'But what follows next; which of these shall govern, and be governed?' 'Is it not clear that the elders should be Governors, and the younger be the governed? And is it not plain, that the best of them should govern?' 'This too is obvious, but aren't the best husbandmen the most assiduous in agriculture?' 'They are, indeed, so, if our Guardians become the best educated, will they not be the most vigilant over the safety of our city? Must we not for this purpose make sure they are prudent, and able, and careful in ruling our city? We must surely do so, for one would need to be most careful in observing what he happens to love. And he will most especially love that which he believes is best for himself, and with those whose good estate he thinks his own is connected. And when he is of a contrary opinion, he will be contrariwise affected.

'We must choose for Guardians such men as shall most of all others, seem to us, on observation, to act with the greatest cheerfulness, through the whole of life, and do whatever they think to be most advantageous for the State, and will never do by any means what appears to be disadvantageous. It seems to me that they ought to be observed through every stage of their life, so that neither temptation nor desire makes them reject this tendency, so that they ought always to do what is best for the State. But some, I think, may have this tendency changed, when grief or agony obliges them to alter course. And those, I imagine you will say, are drawn out of these tendencies, being bewitched by pleasure, or seduced by fear of something or other.' 'It seems that every thing magical can beguile and deceive us.' 'Yes, those qualities which I previously mentioned must be sought, to find out who are the best Guardians, in our opinion and best for the State. And they must be watched from their childhood, setting before them such work in which they will most readily lose any base tendencies of this kind, and become deluded.

'But he who is most mindful, and hard to be deceived, is to be chosen, and he who is otherwise susceptible, is to be rejected. And we must set them trials of endurance and hardship, in which we must watch out for the same qualities. Must we not give them a third trial, that of the magical kind, and watch them as those do, who when they lead young horses against noise and tumult, see whether they are frightened or not? So must they, while still young, be led into difficult tasks, and again be thrown into pleasures, testing them like gold in the fire, in order to see whether such a candidate is difficult to be beguiled with magical tricks, and appears composed amidst all temptation. Thus being a good guardian of himself, protected by that sound harmony in himself, which he has learned from music and gymnastics. So being of such a good character as this, he would truly be of the greatest advantage both to himself and to the State.

'For the man in childhood, in youth, and in manhood, who has been so tried, and who has emerged unsullied, should be appointed Governor and Guardian of the State, and honours be paid to him while he is alive. And when he is dead he should receive the highest reward of a public funeral and a memorial. And he who is not so qualified is to be rejected. Such men of character, Glauco, it seems to me, are to be the best choices for the establishment of our Governors and Guardians. Is it not most just to call these the most complete Guardians, both with reference to our enemies abroad, and to our friends at home, so that the one shall not have the will, nor the other have the power to do any mischief? And the young men, whom we now called Guardians, will be the allies and auxiliaries to the decrees of the Governors.

'What next?' I said, 'I shall attempt, first of all, to persuade the Governors themselves, and the soldiers, and afterwards the rest of the State, that, whatever we educated and instructed them in, then all this advice should be given to them. They should be taught the fable that they were once formed and educated within the Earth, they themselves, their armour and other possessions. And after they were completely fashioned, the Earth, who is their mother, brought them forth, and now they ought to feel affection and gratitude towards the country where they are resident, as to their mother and nurse, and defend her, and to consider the rest of the citizens as being their brothers, sprung from their same Mother Earth.

'But hear the rest of my fable. All of you now in the State are brothers, but the God, when he formed you, mixed gold in the formation of those of you who are able to govern. Therefore they are the most honourable. Furthermore silver in other men are auxiliaries; as are iron and brass in the husbandmen and the other handicrafts. As you are all derived from metal, you resemble one another, and it sometimes happens that from the gold is generated silver, and from the silver there is a gold descendant. The God gives the charge, first of all, chiefly to the Governors and their Guardians, that they will be good, and strongly keep watch over everything, as over their children. Furthermore to know what principles are to be found in their souls, and if their descendants shall be of the brazen or iron kind, they should by no means show diffidence, but grant him honours proportionate to his natural temperament, and shall demote him to the level of craftsmen or husbandmen, if necessary. And if any men and women from among these aspirants shall be born of a gold or silver kind, they shall pay them honour, and promote the golden ones to the Guardianship, and the silver to the auxiliary rank.

'It has been pronounced by the Oracle, that the State is bound to perish when iron or brass has the Guardianship. Have you now any way to persuade them of the truth of this fable?' 'None,' he said, 'to persuade these men themselves, but I shall contrive a way that their sons and posterity, and all mankind afterwards, shall believe it.' 'Even this,' I said, 'would do well towards making them more concerned about the State, and one another, for I understand what you say, and this shall be as the popular voice shall determine. But let us, having armed these Earth-born sons, lead them forwards, led by their Governors, and when they are come into our city, let them consider where is the best place for their camp, so as to keep in order those who are within the city walls. For example, if anyone should want to disobey the laws, or defend the city against those without, or if any enemy, like a wolf, should fall upon the fold.

'And when they have marked out their camp, and performed sacrifices to the proper divinities, let them erect their tents, as many as may be necessary to defend them both from winter and summer weathers?' 'Do you mean houses?' 'Yes, but soldiers' houses, not rich men's.' 'What do you say is the difference between the one and the other?' 'I will try to tell you, for of all things, it is most dreadful, and most shameful to shepherds, to breed such kinds of dogs, as watchers of their flocks, when either through intemperance or famine, or some other ill disposition, the dogs themselves try to hurt the sheep, and, instead of behaving like dogs, resemble wolves. In all truth, we must by all means take care, in case our allies commit such a crime against our citizens, as they are more powerful; and instead of being generous allies, resemble savage dogs.' 'We must take care! Would they not be prepared, as the greater part of that care, if they were really well educated?'

'Well, and so they are,' I replied, 'and that is not worthwhile just to be confidently affirmed, friend Glauco, but it is worthwhile to say, what we are always saying, over and over again, that they ought to have a good education, whatever it is, if they are to receive what is the best result towards making them mild in disposition, both among themselves, and to those who are guarded by them.' 'That's right,' he said, 'besides this good education, anyone of understanding would say that their houses, and all their other buildings, ought to be so constructed, so as not to hinder their Guardians from becoming the very best of men; and not to stir up their fellow citizens to hurt them.'

'Let us consider,' I said, 'how they should live and dwell in some such way as that. First, let none of the Guardians possess any private property, unless there be the very greatest necessity for it. Next, let no citizen own any dwelling, or store-house, into which the Guardian who wishes, may be disallowed from entering. As for the Guardians' necessaries, let them be only temperate, as brave warriors require, and let them arrange with the other citizens, to receive a due reward for their Guardianship, so as to have neither a surplus nor a deficiency of supplies at each year's end. Let them have public meals, as in encampments, and live in common. They must be told that they possess from the Gods the gift of divine gold and divine silver at all times in their souls, and have no need of other human beings for comfort. And that it is profane to pollute the divine gift by mixing it with the ownership of mortal gold, because the money of the vulgar has produced many impious deeds, so that these Guardians remain incorruptible. So, of all the men in the city, they alone are not allowed to handle or touch gold and silver, nor to bring it under their roofs, nor wear it upon themselves, nor drink out of silver or golden goblets. And so they are fit to preserve themselves and the State.

'But if they ever possess lands, and houses, and money, in a private way, they will become stewards and farmers instead of Guardians; hateful lords, instead of the allies of the other citizens, hating and being hated, plotting and being plotted against. Then they shall spend the whole of their lives much oftener and much more afraid of enemies from within, than from without; they and the rest of the State hastening speedily to destruction. For all these reasons,' I said, 'let us make absolutely sure, that our Guardians are so constituted with reference both to their houses and to their other goods. And let us settle these matters by law.

BOOK 4

GOVERNMENT OF
THE REPUBLIC

Adimantus then interjected, 'What, Socrates, will now you say in your own defence, if one should say that you do not make these men very happy, and not by their own fault, for although it is owing to these men that the city really exists, yet they enjoy no advantage in the city, such as others do who possess land, build beautiful and large houses, purchase suitable furniture, offer sacrifices at their own expense, give public entertainments to strangers, and possess gold and silver, and everything which is reckoned to contribute towards making men happy? For one may readily say, that, like hired auxiliaries, they seem to possess nothing in the city, but are only to be employed for keeping watch as Guardians?'

'Yes,' I said, 'and only owning that which is strictly necessary for their maintenance, without receiving, as all others do, any reward. So that they are not allowed even to travel privately anywhere abroad, although they might like to do so; neither may they bestow money on mistresses, nor spend it in such other ways, as those do, who are so called happy. These and many such ordinances you leave out of your accusation against me.' 'So let these things too,' Adimantus said, 'be charged against you.' 'You ask me

Adimantus, what shall I say in our defence? I shall. While we travel on the same road, we shall find, I imagine, what you have said may be also said by many others. And we shall say that there is nothing strange if these men, even in these austere circumstances, should not be the happiest possible in the whole State. Yet it was not with an eye to this that we established the city, to have anyone class in it remarkably happy, beyond the others, but that the whole city might be the happiest on Earth.

'We judged that in such a city, we should most surely find real justice, for injustice in the city is the worst establishment that can happen to it. And that, upon thoroughly examining these principles, we should determine what we have for some time been searching for, the ideal city. Now then, as I imagine, we are forming a happy State, not selecting some few persons to make them alone happy. But we are establishing the universal happiness of the whole population, and we shall next consider a State which is the opposite. As if we were painting human figures, and anyone approaching, might blame us, saying that we do not place the finest colours on the most beautiful parts of the creature; as the eyes, the most beautiful part, are not painted with purple, but with black, should we not apologize sufficiently by saying, "Oh wonderful critic!" Do not imagine that we ought to paint the eyes beautifully, in such a way, as that they would not appear to be the eyes at all; and so with reference to all other parts of the painting.

'But consider, whether, in giving each particular part its due, we make the whole beautiful. And so now, do not oblige us to confer such happiness on our Guardians as shall make them anything other than Guardians. For we know too, how to dress the husbandmen in rich and costly robes, and to encourage them to cultivate the ground only with a view to pleasure, and in like manner, those who make earthenware to lie at their ease by their fire, to drink and feast, neglecting the potter's wheel, and working only so much as they incline. And we know how to confer a felicity of this nature on every individual, in order to render the whole State happy. But do not advise us to act in your manner, Adimantus, since, if we obey you, neither would the husbandman really be a husbandman, nor the potter be a potter; nor would any other citizen really be of any of those professions of which the city is constituted.

'But, as to the others, it is of less consequence, for, when shoemakers become sloppy, and are degenerate, and profess to be shoemakers when they are not, no lasting mischief happens to the State. But when the Guardians of the law and of the State are not true Guardians in reality, but only in appearance, you see how they entirely destroy the whole constitution, if they alone shall have the privilege of an affluent and happy life. If we stand for appointing men who shall be true Guardians of the city, and the least of all harmful to it, then he who makes your objection is for having them to be rather like certain farmers, as in a festival-meeting, not in a city, to be merely content like public entertainers, indulging in jollity and various pleasurable amusements.

'All that hedonism means something quite different from an ideal city. We must seriously consider whether we establish Guardians with this aim in view, that they may bring the greatest happiness for the greatest number, as it pleases the Gods, and we establish them with a view to the happiness of the whole city! Let us see whether this can take place; and let us oblige these auxiliaries and Guardians to do this; and we must persuade them that they shall accordingly become the best performers of their own particular work, and must act towards all others in the same way. And thus the whole city being enhanced, and well constituted, shall allow the several classes to participate in real happiness as their natures permit.

'Let us also consider whether other artificers are corrupted by these things, so as to be made bad workmen.' 'What things do you mean?' 'Riches,' I said, 'and poverty.' 'How?' 'Like this. Does the potter, after he becomes rich, seem likely to go on minding his art? Will he not become idler and more careless than formerly? Will he not become a less skilful potter? And surely, being unable through poverty to furnish himself with tools, or anything else necessary for his craft, his workmanship will be imperfectly executed, and his sons, or those others whom he instructs, will be inferior artists. Through both these influences, poverty and riches, their workmanship in their art is rendered less perfect, and as artists they become less expert. We have, it appears, discovered other dangers, which our Guardians must by all means protect themselves against, and which may in no respect escape their notice, and creep into the city.' 'What kind of things are these?' 'Riches,' I said, 'and poverty; as the one is productive of luxury, idleness, and a love of novelty; and the other, besides a love of novelty, is illiberal, and productive of mischief.'

'They are so, but consider this, Socrates. How shall our city be able to engage in war, since it has little money, especially if she is obliged to wage war against a great opulent state?' 'It is plain,' I said, 'that to fight against an enemy of this kind is somewhat difficult, but to fight against two is a much easier matter. First of all, if they have occasion to fight, will they not, being expert in the art of war, fight against rich men? Well then, Adimantus, don't you think that one boxer, who is fitted out in the best manner possible for this exercise, is easily able to fight against two who are not expert boxers, but, on the contrary, are rich and unwieldy?' 'He would not perhaps easily fight with both at once,' he said. 'Would he not?' I answered, 'although he had it in his power to retreat a little, and then turn on the one who was the nearest to him, and strike him hard, and by doing this frequently in the sun and the heat, might not a person of this kind easily defeat many opponents like these? But don't you think that the rich have more knowledge and experience of boxing than the military art? Easily done then, it is clear; our athletes in combat will double and triple their number.

'But what if they should send an ambassador to another State, informing them of the true state of affairs, telling them, that we make no use of gold or silver, neither is it lawful for us to use them, but with you it is lawful? If you become our allies in the war, you will receive the spoils of all the other States. Do you imagine that any, on hearing these things, would choose to fight against strong and resolute dogs, rather than in alliance with the dogs to fight against fat and tender sheep? But, if the riches of others be amassed into one State, we must see that it does not endanger those who are poor. You are content that you imagine any other State deserves to be called a State, besides such a one as we have established? We must give to the others,' said I, 'a more magnificent name than mere State, if each of them consists of many States, and is not one, such as the Republic.

'It is like a game, for there are always in States, two parties at war with each other, the poor and the rich. And in each of these parties, there are very many individuals, which if you treat them as one group, you are entirely mistaken. But, if you regard them as many, you put one part of them in possession of the goods, and give the power to another, or even deliver up the one to the other. You shall always have the majority for your allies, and the minority for enemies, and, as long as your State shall continue harmoniously, as it is now established, it shall be the greatest. I do not say it shall be recorded as such, but it shall be really the greatest, though its defenders were no more than one thousand. For one State so great as ours, you will not easily find, either among the Greeks or Barbarians, but only many States, which are counted to be many times larger than ours.

'Might not this be the best guide for our rulers to decide how large to make the city, and to what extent to mark off ground for it, in proportion to its bulk, without paying attention to anything else? I think that so long as the city, when it is on its increase, continues to be one, so it may be increased, but not beyond it. Shall we not then place this further injunction on our Guardians, to take care, by all means, that the city be neither thought to be small nor great, but to be of moderate size, and to remain as one city?' 'We shall probably,' said he, 'consider that a trifling affair.'

'A more trifling affair still is, as we mentioned before, when we observed that if any descendant of the Guardians be depraved, he ought to be demoted to the labouring classes, and if any descendant of the labouring classes be found worthy, he is to be raised to the rank of the Guardians. This, I believe, was intended to show that all the citizens ought to apply themselves to that particular art for which he or she has a natural genius, and the whole State would become unified. We do not,' I said, 'good Adimantus, as you may imagine, consult in many and great matters, but only in those which are merely trifling. However, if they take care of one grand point, as the saying goes, or rather that which is sufficient in place of the grand, that is sufficient.' 'What is that?' he said. 'Education!' I said, 'and nurture. For if, being well educated, they become temperate men, they will easily see through all these matters, and other possibilities that we shall omit at present, regarding women, marriages, and the propagation of the species. For these affairs ought all, according to the proverb, be shared, as being held in common among friends.

'And surely,' I said, 'if once a State is really established, it proceeds happily, increasing like a circle. And while sound education and nurture are preserved, they produce good natures; and good natures, partaking of such education, produce offspring with still better natures. This is true in other respects, not only with reference to propagation, as is the case with other animals. To state it briefly, that the Guardians of the State must hold fast, so that nothing may escape their notice and be impaired. Above all things, they must guard against this error, and not make any innovations in the curricula of gymnastics and music, contrary to the established order of the State. But to maintain this order as much as possible; being afraid that when it is said, "Men most admire that song, which most partakes of novelty" one should not by any chance imagine that the poet means new songs, but a new method of playing the song. Such a novelty is not to be commended, for, to receive a new kind of music is to be guarded against, as endangering the whole of the constitution; for never should the measures of music be altered without affecting the great laws of the constitution, according to Damon, with whom I agree.

'We must erect,' I said, 'some barrier, somewhere here, for our Guardians themselves, in regard to music. A transgression here easily steals in imperceptibly. By becoming familiar by degrees, it insensibly moves into manners and pursuits, and from there, into the way of relating, the one to another. It spreads, and from this interchange, enters into laws and policies with great impudence, until at last it overturns everything worthwhile, both in private and public life. Decadent music creates a decadent culture, discordant music creates discordant minds, corrupted music creates more corruption and so on.

'Ought not our children, as I said at the beginning, receive directly from their infancy an education conforming to the laws of the constitution? Because, if their education be such as is contrary to law, and the children be of such a nature themselves, it is impossible that they should ever grow up to be worthy men and women, observant of the laws. For when beguiling amusements are thrust on them from their infancy, and when, by means of their music, they embrace that amusement which, according to law, is contrary to harmonious music, it is harmful. Wholesome music should accompany them in every activity, and grow with them. It raises up in the city whatever formerly has fallen down. And these young men discover those rules which appeared trifling, and which others have destroyed.' 'What rules?' 'Such as keeping silence by the younger before the elder, which is good manners; giving them priority of place, rising up before them, and having great reverence for parents. Likewise they should learn clean shaving, and what clothes and shoes are proper in which to clothe their bodies, and everything else of that kind.

'But to establish these things by law, would, I imagine, be foolish and futile, for it isn't done anywhere in the world, nor would it stand up in practice, although established both by word and in writing. It seems, Adimantus, that a man's character and conduct will always be according to his education, let him apply himself afterwards to what he will. For, does not the like always produce the like? And we may say at last that a sound education arrives at some result which is complete, vigorous, and good. Bad education results in the opposite. I would not then, for these reasons, undertake to settle by law such affairs as these.

'But now, by Zeus, we must be willing to consider those laws relative to matters of commerce, and to their traffic one with another in the market. And their traffic among handicrafts here, leading to scandals, bodily harm, raising of lawsuits, the institution of judges, and the imposts and payment of taxes, either in the market or at ports. In general whatever laws are needed, municipal, civil, or marine. Shall we dare to establish any of these?' 'It is improper,' he said, 'to prescribe these to good and worthy men; for they will easily find out most of them, those that ought to be established by law, for themselves.' 'Yes,' I said, 'friend, if at least God grants them the preservation of the laws we formerly explained. And if not, they may spend the whole of their lives making and amending such laws as these, imagining that they shall attain to that which is best.'

'You say that there are the uneducated, and those who are sick, and at the same time unwilling, through intemperance, to quit an unwholesome diet, which is injurious to the good of the State. That is so, and a pleasant life these should live too! For, though they deal with physicians, they gain nothing, but render their diseases greater and more complex, and they still hope, that when anyone recommends any medicine to them, they shall by means of it be made whole. This is entirely the situation of such diseased persons. But isn't this agreeable to them?; to see that the man is most hateful of all, who tells them the truth, that, until one gives up drunkenness and gluttony, unchaste pleasures, and laziness, then neither drugs, caustics, amputations, charms, applications, medicines, or any other such prescriptions as these, will be of any use.' 'That,' he said, ' is unpleasant, for we become enraged at one who tells us what is right and has nothing pleasant about it.' 'You are no admirer,' I said, 'it would seem, of this kind of man?' 'No, truly.'

'Then, though the whole of the city, do such degenerate acts! Would you commend them? Or, is not the same offence which is done by these people, done by all those other cities, which, being ill-governed, encourage their citizens not to alter any part of the constitution. Furthermore any degenerate who commit such deeds is to be put to death. But, whosoever shall with the greatest cheerfulness, reverence those who govern, and gratifies them in the most humble manner, anticipating their desires, and is most dexterous in satisfying them, shall be reckoned both worthy and wise in matters of highest importance. And he shall be held by them in the greatest respect?

'And again, as for all those who desire to serve such States, and are even fond of it, are you not delighted with their courage and skill?' 'I am; except if they obey such rules imposed on them by the multitude, and fancy they are really good politicians, because they are commended by the mob.' 'How do you mean? Do you find excuses for such men?' I said, 'or do you even think it is possible for a man who cannot himself measure height, when he hears many other men equally ignorant, telling him that he is six feet high, not to believe this of himself? It is impossible not to be disapproving in this case, for such men as these are of all men, the most ridiculous. They are always making laws about such matters as we now mentioned, and always amending them. They imagine that they shall find some period when frauds in commerce, and those other deceits I have spoken about, can be stopped forever, being ignorant that they are in reality attempting to destroy a hydra!

'I believe,' I said, 'that a true lawgiver ought not to disturb himself overmuch, about such a type of law and government, either in an ill or well-regulated state. In the one, because it is unprofitable and of no avail, in the other, because anyone can find out some of the laws, and others of them flow naturally from the habits arising from their early education.' 'What part, then, of the institutions of law have we yet remaining?' I replied, 'That to us indeed there is nothing remaining; but, to the Delphic Oracle there remains the greatest, noblest, and most important of legal institutions. The institutions of temples, sacrifices, and other worship of the Gods, dæmons, and heroes. Also the disposing of the dead, and whatever rites ought to be performed over them, so as to make them propitious. For truly such ceremonies as these, we ourselves neither know, nor, in founding the State, will we entrust them to any other party. If we are wise, we will not we make use of any other interpreter, except the Delphic Oracle. For this oracle is the interpreter in every country to all men in these matters, who interprets them, sitting in the centre of the Earth. And it is well established, by honoured and time-proven tradition that we must act accordingly.

'So, now, dear son of Aristo, that is the ideal city to be established for you. And, at our next place of meeting, having procured sufficient candlelight, please call on your brother and on Polemarchus and the others to assist us, to discover if by any means, may perceive where justice rules, and where injustice lies. And in what respect they differ from each other, and which of them the man should acquire, who desires to be happy, whether he be concealed, or not concealed, both from Gods and men.' 'But you, Socrates, say nothing to that purpose,' replied Glauco, 'for you yourself promised to enquire into this, thinking it was impious of you not to assist the cause of justice by every possible means.'

BOOK 5

EDUCATION OF THE
PHILOSOPHER

'I believe that both this model city and republic, and such a Guardian as we have described, who is good and upright to ensure that this republic remains an upright one, is truly just. I believe that any of the other ways to govern the city are bad and miss the mark, both as to the regulation of the city, and establishing the good temperament of the soul of its citizens; and that there are four kinds of depravity.'

I was then starting to mention them in order, as they seemed to me to rise out of one another, but Polemarchus, stretching out his hand, as he sat a little further away from Adimantus, caught him by the robe at his shoulder, and drew him near. Then bending towards him, said something in a whisper, of which we heard nothing but this, 'Shall we let that pass then, or what shall we do?' 'Not at all,' said Adimantus, speaking out aloud. And I replied, 'What will you not let pass?' 'You,' he said. 'And which of my remarks in particular do you mean?' 'You seem to us to be growing negligent,' he said, 'and to steal a whole branch of the discourse from discussion, and that is quite considerable, so that you may not have the trouble of going through it.

'Furthermore you imagine that you escaped our notice, when you simplified this matter. For example, that as to wives and children, you said that it is obvious to everyone, that these offspring will be held in common among friends.' 'Didn't I speak correctly then, Adimantus?' 'Yes,' he said, 'but this word "right", like other parts of your discourse, requires some explanation, to show what is the precise way that they are being brought up in common, for there may be many ways of doing it. So, do not omit to tell us what is the method you refer to, for we have been waiting for some time thinking you would, on some occasion, make mention of the propagation of children. In what way they should be parented, and, when they are born, how they should be nurtured. And everything relative to what you said concerning wives and children being held in common. For we believe, that it is of the utmost importance to the State, when this is rightly performed, or otherwise it will be to its detriment. But now, you are entering on the consideration of another constitution, before you have sufficiently discussed these matters. It therefore seems proper to us that what I have said should not be allowed to pass, before you go over all these matters, as you did the others.'

'And you may count on me too,' said Glauco, 'as joining in this vote.' 'You may easily see, dear Socrates,' said Thrasymachus, 'that this is the opinion of us all.' 'What is this,' I said, 'that you have done, taking hold of me like that? What a mighty long discourse you now raise, as you did at the beginning, about a republic, in which I was rejoicing at having now been completed, being pleased with any one of you who would have let things pass, and being content with whatever was said! But you do not know what a swarm of arguments you raise, by your challenge, which I foreseeing, passed by at that time, in case it should cause great disturbance.'

'What then,' said Thrasymachus, 'do you imagine that we have now come here hunting for gold, and not to hear your reasoning?' 'Yes,' I said, 'but in due course.' 'The whole of life, Socrates,' said Glauco, 'is known by the wise, along with the right measure of hearing such arguments as these. But pass by what relates to us, and do not grudge to explain your opinion concerning the current object of our enquiry, which is what kind of community of wives and children is to be observed by our Guardians; and concerning the nurture of the latter while they are very young, in the time between their birth and their formal education, which seems to be the most difficult time of all. Endeavour to tell us in what manner it should be done, please Socrates.'

'It is not easy, dear Glauco,' I said, 'to go through these matters for they raise more doubts than any, about all of which we have already spoken. It might not be believed that this should be possible, and although it might easily be achieved, whether it would be for the best might still be doubted. Therefore, dear companions, I am somewhat reluctant to touch on these matters, in case our reasoning appears to be rather a pious hope, than what could actually take place.' 'Do not be reluctant,' said Glauco, 'for your listeners are neither stupid, nor incredulous, nor ill-affected towards you.' 'Then,' I said, 'do you say this, most excellent Glauco, with a desire to encourage me?' 'I do,' he said.

'Then your speech has a quite contrary effect for, if I trusted to myself, that I understood what I am to say, your encouragement would do well. For one who understands the truth about the greatest and the most interesting matters, must speak with safety and confidence among the wise and friendly. But to be diffident in oneself, and doubtful of the truth, and at the same time to be haranguing you as I do now, is both wrong and dangerous, in case it should be exposed to ridicule. For although this may all be a trifling matter, but perhaps in mistaking the truth, I not only fail myself, but draw my friends along with me into an error about matters in which we ought least of all to be mistaken. I therefore crave the pardon of Nemesis, for the sake of what, Glauco, I am going to say. For I trust it is a smaller offence to be a man-slayer without intention, than to be an impostor with regard to what is good and excellent, just and lawful. And it would be better to risk such an attempt among enemies than friends, as you give me some encouragement.'

'Then, Socrates,' Glauco said, laughing, 'if we allow anything amiss from your discourse, we shall be unable to acquit you of any man-slaughter, and as an impostor. So proceed boldly!' 'But indeed,' I said, 'he who is acquitted at a court of justice is cleared of the crime, as the law says, and if it be so in that case, it is reasonable it should be so in this.' 'As for that,' Glauco said, 'please now proceed.' 'We must now return again to what, it seems, according to the correct method of discourse, should have been stated before.

'So perhaps it is right to proceed in this manner, that, after having entirely finished the curricula respecting the men, we now go over all that which concerns the women, especially since you challenge me to proceed in this manner. For, in my opinion, men who have been well born and well educated in such a manner as we have described, should not have the rightful possession and enjoyment of children and wives, but should be only pursuing the single aim, from which we proceeded in the beginning. For we have endeavoured, in our reasoning, to form men as the true Guardians of the State. Let us proceed, and establish similarly, certain rules relating to the propagation and nurture of children.

'So, let us first consider whether they are correct or not. I mean as to whether we should judge it proper for the females of our Guardians to be observant in the same manner as the males are, and to guard along with them, and do everything else in common. Or shall we judge it proper for them to manage domestic affairs within doors, as being unsuitable for the other exercises? In other words, just giving birth, and the nursing of the children, while the males labour, and have the whole care of the citizens.' 'They should do all that,' he said, 'entirely sharing in common. Only we are to remember the females are physically the weaker sex, and the males as the stronger sex, when we employ them.'

'But is it possible to employ any creature for the same purpose as another, unless you give it the same nurture and education as you give to the other? If then we shall employ the women for the same purposes as we do the men, must we not also give them the same education? Were not music and gymnastics given to the males? These two arts therefore, and those relating to war, must be given also to the women, and they must be employed with concern about the same matters. Yet as these proposals are contrary to custom, many of these suggestions we are now speaking about may appear to be ridiculous, if practised in the way we mention.

'What,' said I, 'do you see as the most ridiculous part? Is it not plain that you could see the women wrestling naked in the Palæstra along with the men, and not only the young women, but even the more advanced in years, in the same manner as old men in the wrestling schools, when they are wrinkled, and not at all handsome to the eye, yet are still fond of their exercises?

'Must we not therefore', I said, 'since we have embarked upon this discourse, be afraid of the railleries of the men of gallantry, whatever words they may say with regard to such a revolution being introduced, as well as in gymnastics as in music, and particularly in the use of arms, and riding on horseback? But since we have started on this discourse, we must go to the extremity of the law, and beg these men not to follow their own customs, but to think seriously, and remember, that it is not so long ago since these activities appeared base and ridiculous to the Greeks, which are now so only to most of the Barbarians; such as to see naked men. And when first the Cretans, and afterwards the Lacedæmonians, began their exercises, it was in the power of the men of humour, of that time, to turn all these notions into ridicule.

'But I imagine that when, by experience, it appeared better to strip themselves of all these notions than to be wrapped up in them, and they were removed by the idea of the best examples, indicated by reasoning. And this too showed manifestly, that he is a fool who believes anything to be ridiculous except that which is obviously bad, and attempts to settle upon any other idea of the ridiculous, but that of the foolish and the vicious, or to be serious in any other pursuit but that of the Good. Isn't the first principle of all to be agreed upon, is whether this notion of holding all things in common, is possible or not? And we must allow an opportunity for dispute, if anyone, either in jest or in earnest, inclines to doubt, whether the human nature in the female sex is able, in every way, to bear an equal share with the male? Or if it be not in any one thing? Or if it be able in some things, but not in others? And among which of these are in the affairs of war, and which in the ways of peace? Would not the man who sets out this question in the most objective manner conclude too, most objectively?

'Are you all willing, that we ourselves, on behalf of the others, dispute about these things, while the opposite side may be deprived of a defence?' 'Nothing should hinder us in the pursuit of truth,' Glauco said. 'Let us say that there is no need, for I, Socrates, and you Glauco, and others, to dispute about this matter. For you yourselves in the beginning of our discourse, when we established our city, agreed that it was necessary for each individual to practise one work, according to their different dispositions. I think we agreed why it would be bad if they did not? Does not the physical nature of the male differ widely from that of the female? Surely it differs a great deal. Only an idiot would think they were the same. And is it not right to encourage each to different work, according to their nature?

'Are you not in the wrong now, and contradicting yourselves, when you say that men and women ought to do the same things, whilst their nature is extremely different? Can you in answer to these solid objections, my good friends, make any defence?' 'It is not such a simple matter,' he said, 'to do it immediately, but I will entreat you, and do now entreat you, to go through the arguments on our side, whatever they may be.' 'These are the consequences, Glauco,' I replied, 'and many others, which long ago I foresaw, and was therefore both afraid and backward in touching on the law concerning the possession of wives, and the education of children.

'It is indeed not easy,' I said, 'but the case is clear. If a man falls into a small fish-pond, or into the middle of the greatest sea, he must still swim in the one, no less than in the other. Must we then swim, and endeavour to escape from this reasoning, expecting that either some dolphin is to lift us out, or that we shall have some other remarkable deliverance?

Come then, let us see if we can anywhere find an exit, for we do acknowledge that different natures ought to study different things, and the nature of men and women are obviously different.

'How fine, Glauco,' I said, 'is the power of the art of contradiction! Because, many seem to fall into this trap unwillingly, and imagine that they are reasoning correctly. They are cavilling, because they are unable to understand the subject, by dividing it into its proper divisions, and will propose a set of verbal contradictions of some statement or other, making trivial objections instead of sound reasoning.' 'This may be, the case with many,' he said, 'but does it presently apply to us?' 'Entirely so,' I said, 'we seem unwillingly to have fallen into a quarrel about words, because you have very strenuously resisted the substance of the statement, that when the nature is not the same, they ought not to have the same employments. But we have not yet, in any respect, considered what is the characteristic of that sameness or diversity of nature, or to what it points. We stopped when we assigned different pursuits to different natures, and to the same natures the same pursuits.

'It is therefore, still in our power to question ourselves, whether the nature of the bald, or of those who wear their hair, are the same, or different? And after that we should agree that it was different, whether, if the bald made shoes, we should allow those who wear hair to also make shoes? Or, if those who wear hair made them, whether we should allow the others to make them?' 'That is ridiculous, your sense of irony has got the better of you, once again,' he replied. 'Is it in any other respect,' I said, 'more ridiculous than that we did not wholly determine the sameness and diversity of different natures, but attended only to those kinds of diversity and sameness with respect to their employments; just as we say that one physician and another have one and the same nature? Don't you think so?' 'I do.' 'That the physician and architect have a different nature.' 'Entirely.'

'And so,' I replied, 'concerning the fundamentally different natures of men and of women. If they appear to be different, in respect to any art, or other employment, we will say that this different employment is to be assigned to each separately. But if their natures appear different only in this respect, that the female brings forth, and the male begets, we shall not say that this has at all shown the man to be different from the woman, in the respect of which we speak. But we shall still be of the opinion that both our Guardians and their wives ought to pursue the same employments. Shall we not henceforth insist that anyone who says the opposite is only to instruct us on this point. What is that art or work, with respect to the establishment of a city, where the nature of the man and woman is not the same, but different?

'Possibly, someone might say, as you were saying some time since, that it is not easy to reason about this sufficiently all of a sudden, but that it is easy for one who has previously considered it. Are you willing that we desire such an opponent to listen to us, if by any means we can show him that there is in the administration of the city no employment that is just peculiar to the women? Isn't this your meaning? That one man has a good genius for one thing, and another bad, in this respect, that one can learn anything easily, and the other with great difficulty. And the one with just a little instruction discovers much in what he learns, but the other, even when he obtains a great deal of instruction and care, does not retain very much of what he has learned.

'With the one, the body is duly subservient to the mind,

but with the other, it opposes its improvement. Are there any marks other than these by which you would determine one to have a good genius for anything, and another to have a bad one? Do you know of any concern which is managed by mankind, with reference to which the men have not all these marks in a more excellent degree than the women? Or, should we not be tedious, if we mentioned particularly the weaving art, and the dressing pot-herbs and victuals, in which the female genius seems to be somewhat superior?' 'You speak truly,' he said, 'that in general, as in most things, the one sex is superior to the other, yet there are very many women who in many things excel many men, but, on the whole, it is as you say.'

'There is not, my friend, any office among the whole inhabitants of the city peculiar to the woman, considered solely for a woman, and not for a man, and the natural aptitudes are indiscriminately diffused through both. The woman may be naturally fitted for sharing in all offices, and so is the man, but overall the woman is physically much weaker than the man. Shall we commit everything to the care of the men, and nothing to the care of the women? It is therefore, I imagine, like this, that one woman too, is fitted by natural genius to become a physician, and another is not. One is naturally a musician, and another is not, and one is naturally fitted for gymnastics, and another is not. One is fitted for war, and another is not. And is not one likewise a lover of philosophy, and another averse to it; one of high spirits, and another of low morale?

'And has not one woman a natural genius for being a Guardian, and another has not? Did we not make a choice of such qualities as these for our Guardian men? The nature of the woman and of the man for the Guardianship of the city is the same, only that the one is physically weaker, and the other stronger. And such women as these are to be chosen to live with these men, and be Guardians along with them, as they are naturally fit companions for them, and of a kindred genius. And must not the same employments be assigned to the same natures?

'We have now arrived by a circular progression concerning all that we formerly mentioned, and, we allow that it is not contrary to nature to appoint the wives of our Guardians to study both music and gymnastics. We are not then establishing an impossible state of affairs, like a pious hope, since we establish the law according to nature, and what is at present contrary to these arrangements, is contrary to nature. Was not our enquiry to learn, whether our proposals are both possible and the best? And we have agreed that these things are possible. And so we must next agree that if they are best, it is clear that we must agree that in order to make a woman a Guardian, the education should not be different from that of the men, especially as she has the same natural genius.

'What do you think then of such an opinion as this? That of thinking that one man is better, and another worse, or do you think them to be all alike? In the city now which we are to establish, do you judge that our Guardians with this fine education we have described, or shoemakers with a sound education in their craft, will be made the better men?' 'That question,' he replied, 'is ridiculous.' 'I understand you,' I said, 'but of all the other citizens, are not the Guardians the best? But will not these women Guardians too be the best of women? Is there anything better in a city than that both the women and the men are educated to be the very best? This then will be effected by music and gymnastics, being taught to them according to the curricula we have described.

'We have then established a law which is not only possible, but moreover best for the State. The wives of our Guardians must be unclothed, since instead of clothes they will wear virtue as their dress [laughter], and they must bear a part in war, and take part in the other duties of Guardianship of the city, and do nothing else. But the lightest part of these services is to be allotted to the women rather than to the men, on account of the physical weakness of their sex. And the man who laughs at naked women, while performing the exercises for the sake of what is best, reaps the empty fruit of a ridiculous wisdom, and in no respect knows, as it seems, at what he laughs, nor why he does it. For that ever was and will be thought to be a noble saying, that what is profitable is beautiful, and what is hurtful is base.'

'By all means, let us say,' he said, 'that we have escaped one ocean wave, as it were, having thus settled the law with respect to the women, without being wholly overwhelmed, ordaining that our male and female Guardians are to manage all things in common, and our reasoning has been consistent with itself, as it respects both what is possible and likewise advantageous. It is truly no small sea wave we have escaped.' 'You will not,' I replied, 'call it a great one, when you see what follows. That law, and those others formerly mentioned imply, as I think, the following. That these women must all be available in common to all these men, and that no one woman should dwell with any man privately, and that their children likewise be held in common, and that the parent should not know his own children, nor the children know their parent. This is much greater than the other arrangement, as to its incredibility, both of it being possible, and at the same time advantageous.'

'I do not believe,' he replied, 'that anyone will doubt its utility, at least, as if it were not the greatest good to have the women and children in common, if it were at all possible. But I think the greatest question will be, whether it is possible or not? And one may very readily argue as to both possibilities.' 'You mention,' I replied, 'a possibility of numerous disputes. But I thought that I should at least have escaped from that one, if its utility had already been agreed upon, and that it should have only remained for us to consider its possibility.' 'But you have not,' he said, 'escaped unobserved, give then an account of both possibilities.' 'I must then,' I said, 'submit to a trial, however, indulge me so far.

'Allow me to indulge myself, as those are inclined to glut themselves who are sluggish in their mind, when they walk alone. For men of this type, sometimes, before they find out how they shall gain what they desire, waive that enquiry, so that they may not tire themselves in deliberating about the possibility or impossibility of it; and suppose they have obtained what they desire, and then go through what remains. And they delight in running over what they will do when their desire is obtained, rendering their soul, otherwise indolent to be more indolent still. I am now sympathetic after this manner, and wish to defer these debates, and to enquire afterwards whether these things are actually possible or not. But at present, holding them as possible, if you allow me, I will consider in what manner our rulers shall regulate these arrangements, when they take place, that they may be executed in the most advantageous manner, both for the State and for the Guardians.

'These matters I shall endeavour, in the first place, to go over with your assistance, and the others afterwards, if you will allow me. I think,' I said, 'that if our rulers are worthy of that name, and in a similar manner, those who are their auxiliaries as their ministers in the government, that the latter will be disposed to do whatever is asked of them, and the former will be ready to command. As they pay direct obedience to the law in general, and follow the spirit of the law in whatever matters are left to them to carry out.

'Whoever is their lawgiver, in the same way as you have chosen from the men, you should choose similarly from the women, accepting that their different talents are as equal as possible. And as they are to dwell and dine together in common, and as no one possesses any goods privately, they will all live happily together. And combining in their exercises and other diversions, they will be led from an innate necessity, as is natural, to enjoy sexual intercourse one with the other. I do not mean to say that will necessarily happen but it will probably happen.' 'Not,' he replied, 'by any friendly, but amatory necessity, which seems to be more powerful than the other, to persuade and draw the bulk of mankind together.' 'Much more,' I said, 'but after this probability, Glauco, to mix together, or to do anything else, in a disorderly manner, is unlawful in a city of contented persons, nor will the rulers permit it.

'It is plain, that after this licentious probability we must make marriage, as much as possible a sacrament, and the most advantageous custom would be for it to be considered the most sacred. How will they keep to their relationship as being sacred, and as the most advantageous? Tell me that, Glauco, for I see in your houses dogs of chase, and a great many excellent birds. Have you indeed ever attended at all, in any respect, to their marriages, and the propagation of their species? First of all, that among these men and women, although they be excellent in themselves, are there not some who are more excellent? How do you breed from all of them alike? Or are you careful to breed chiefly from the best?' 'From the best.' 'But how? From the youngest or from the oldest, or from those who are most in their prime?' 'From those most in their prime.' 'And if the breed is not of this kind, do you reckon that the race of birds and dogs greatly degenerates?' 'I reckon so,' he replied. 'And what do you think about horses,' I said, 'and other animals, is the case any different with respect to these?' 'That,' he said, 'is absurd.'

'Strange,' I said, 'my dear friend! What extremely perfect Governors we must have, if the case be the same with respect to the whole human race!' 'However, it is so,' he replied. 'But why is it so?' 'Because there is a necessity,' I replied, 'for their using many medicines. For where bodies have no need of medicines, but are ready to subject themselves to a regimen of diet, we reckon that a weak physician may be sufficient, but when there is a necessity for medicines, we know that a more able physician is then required.' 'True, but with what in view do you say this, which is relevant to our discussion?' 'With this in view,' I replied. 'It appears that our rulers are obliged to use a great deal of fiction and deceit, for the advantage of the governed, and we said previously, that all these devices were useful in the same way as medicine.

'This now seems not to be the most important factor in marriages, and the propagation of children. It is better,' I said, 'from what we have already acknowledged, that the best men desire sexual intercourse, for the most part, with the best women. And the most depraved men, on the contrary, desire the most depraved women. And the offspring of the former are to be educated, but not that of the latter, if you desire to have a people of the best kind. And this sexual coming together, must be performed in such a manner as to escape the notice of all but the Governors themselves, if you would have the whole flock of the Guardians to be free from sedition as possible.

'Shall there not be some festivals established by law, in which we shall draw together all the prospective brides and bridegrooms? Sacrifices too must be performed, and hymns composed by our poets suitable to the marriages which we are making. But the number of the marriages is to be decided by the rulers, that as much as possible, they may preserve the same number of men, having an eye to coming wars, diseases, and everything else of this kind. And that as far as possible, our city should grow to be neither too great nor too little. And certain arrangements too, I imagine, should be made so cleverly, that the depraved man may, on every sexual encounter, blame his ill fortune, and not the Governors.

'And those of the youth who distinguish themselves, whether in war or anywhere else, must have rewards and prizes given them, and the most ample freedom of having sexual intercourse with the finest women, that so, under this pretext, the greatest number of children may be born from these best persons. And shall the children always, as they are born, be received by magistrates appointed for these purposes to be registered, whether boys or girls? For the magistrates are held in common for females as for males. And when they receive these children of the most worthy persons, they will carry them, I imagine, to the nursery, to certain nurses dwelling apart in a certain district of the city. But the children of the more depraved, and such others as are in any way maimed, they will hide in some secret and obscure place, as is necessary, if they want the breed of the Guardians to remain pure.

'And shall they similarly take care of their nursing, in bringing to the nursery the mothers when their breasts are full of milk, practising every art, so that no one knows her own child, and in using the others who have milk, if the former shall prove insufficient? And they shall also take care of these nurses, that they suckle for a competent time; and they shall appoint the nurses and housekeepers to be watchful, and to take on every other necessary work.' 'You speak,' said he, 'of great luxury for the wives of our Guardians, in their breeding of children.' 'It is necessary,' I replied, 'but let us now be more serious and discuss that topic which we chiefly intended.

'We said that the best offspring should be born to persons in their prime. Are you then of the opinion with me, that the proper season of vigour is twenty years for a woman, and thirty for a man?' 'What continuance is there to these seasons?' he asked. 'The woman,' I answered, 'beginning at twenty, is to bear children for the State until the age of forty, and the man, after he has passed the most flourishing part of his fertility, from that period, is to sire children for the State until the age of fifty-five. If anyone who is older or younger than these men and women shall meddle in generating children for the general public, we shall say that this trespass is neither lawful nor just, because he presents to the State a child, which, if it is concealed, is born and grows up not from sacrifices and prayers, (which the priestesses and priests, and the whole of the city, shall offer in thanks, that the descendants of the good may still be better, and from their useful descendants still more excellent progeny may arise). But a child conceived in darkness, is usually not temperate.

'And the law,' I said, 'must be the same for those men who

are not yet of the age ripe for generating children, shall not have sexual intercourse with women, also of the proper age, without the permission of the magistrate. And I imagine, that when the women and men exceed the age of generating, we shall permit the men to cohabit with any woman they wish, besides their daughter and mother of course. As well as those who are the children of their daughters, or parents of their mother. Similarly the women may not have intercourse with a son or father, and the children of these, or their parents. All this freedom we will allow them, after we have encouraged them to attend carefully, in the first place, to the situation that if any child should be conceived, and not brought into the light, and if conceived by any accident, it should be brought forward, to be exposed as a child for which no provision has been made.'

'All these arrangements,' he said, 'are reasonable. But how shall fathers and daughters, and those other relations you have now mentioned, be known to one another?' 'They shall not be known at all,' I said, 'but from the day on which any one of them is a bridegroom or bride, whatever children are born in the tenth to the seventh month after the wedding, they shall call the males their sons, and the females their daughters, and they shall call him father, and her mother. And in the same way again, they shall call the children of these marriages their grandchildren, and they again shall call them grandfathers and grandmothers. And those who were born in that period in which their fathers and mothers were conceiving children, they shall call their sisters and brothers, so as not to have sexual relations with each other, as I just now pronounced. But the law shall allow brothers and sisters to live together, if the Pythian Oracle gives consent.

'That, Glauco, and such arrangements as these, will form

the community of women and children, among our city Guardians, and that it is consistent with the other parts of our polity, and by far the best. We must, in the next place, establish all these arrangements from the standpoint of reason? Did we not agree on this at the very beginning? To enquire what we consider to be the greatest good with relation to the establishment of a State, with an eye to which the lawgiver should enact the laws. And what is the greatest evil? And then to enquire, whether what we have already decided contributes towards leading us in the steps of the Good, and away from that of evil?

'Is there, any greater evil in a city than that which lacerates it, and, instead of one unity, makes it into a multiplicity? Or, is there any greater good than that which binds it together, and makes it one? Does not the sharing of pleasure and pain bind them together, when all of the citizens, as far as possible rejoice and mourn in the same way, for those blessings when they are obtained, and when they are lost? But a separate feeling concerning these events destroys it. That is when some of the citizens are extremely grieved, and others extremely glad, at exactly the same happenings in the city, and of those who are in it. Does not such an evil arise from this, when all of them don't jointly in the State pronounce these words, "mine", and "not mine" in agreement?

'And will not that city be best regulated, when every individual, with regard to the concerns of another, in the same way, pronounce these words, "mine", and "not mine" together? And it is such a city that comes nearest to the condition of a single man in unity. As when our finger is somehow hurt, the whole painful feeling spreads throughout the body, and to the soul. One co-ordination of its governing part, perceives it, and the entire whole grieves along with the distressed part. So we say that the man is distressed in his finger, and that realization is felt the same way, as to any other part of a man, both with respect to grief, when any part is in pain, or with respect to pleasure, when any part is at ease.

'And to return to your question, the city which comes nearest to this ideal, is governed in the best manner, and when any one of the citizens receives any good or suffers any ill, such a city, I imagine, will most especially say, that she herself accepts it as one, and the whole city rejoices or grieves together. It may be time for us to go back to considering our city, and reflect on how those arrangements in which we have agreed on, in our reasoning, as to whether they prevail most in our city or more in some other.

'What now? Are there not, in other cities, Governors and people? And are there not similarly in this city? And will not all these call one another citizens? But besides this concerning the citizens, what do the people call their Governors in other States?' 'Masters or Lords in most States, and, in Democracies, this very name, Governors.' 'But in our city, besides that of citizens, what do the people call their Governors?' 'Their Preservers,' said he, 'and Helpers.' 'And what do they call the people?' 'Rewarders,' he replied, 'and Nourishers.' 'And in other cities, what do the Governors call their people?' 'Slaves,' he replied. 'And what do the Governors call one another?' 'Fellow Rulers,' he said. 'And in ours, what shall they call them?' 'Fellow Guardians.' 'Can you tell, whether any one of the Governors in other cities can address one of their fellow Governors as his kinsman, and another as a stranger?' 'Very many so.' 'Does he not reflect and call the kindred one his own, and the stranger one as not his own?'

'But how is it with our Guardians? Is there so much as any one of them who can think of calling any one of their fellow Guardians a stranger? For, with whomever anyone meets, he reckons he meets with a brother or sister, a father or mother, a son or daughter, or the descendants or ancestors of these.' 'You speak well,' I replied. 'But furthermore, tell me this in addition, whether you will establish among them by law, the use of these kindred names? Or will you just encourage them to perform all their actions in conformity with these names?' 'With respect to parents, whatever the law states is to be performed by parents, such as reverence, and care, and obedience. Otherwise it will not be to his advantage, either in the sight of the Gods or of men, if he acts in any way which is either unlawful or unjust in any actions accompanying them.' 'Of all cities, there will be the greatest harmony here.

'Will not our citizens especially possess in common that which they call their own; and, sharing all things and affections in common, they will of all affections most especially have in common pleasure and pain? And along with the other parts of the constitution, is not the community of women and children among the Guardians the cause of these benefits? So we agreed, that this was the greatest Good for the city, comparing a well established city to a body, in it being affected by the pleasure and pain of any one of its parts. This community, of women and children among our auxiliaries, has appeared to us to be the cause of the greatest Good to the city. And surely we agree at least with what we said before, that they ought not to own houses of their own, nor land, nor any possessions. But, receiving their subsistence from others, as a reward for their Guardianship, they should all share it in common, if they intend really to be good Guardians.

'Both these arrangements were formerly mentioned, and now we speak of them again, so that makes them real Guardians, and prevents the city from being injured, by their not calling any possessions their own, one owning one thing, and one another thing. One taking to his own house whatever he can possess, separate from the others; and another to his own house, which is different from the others, but both having different wives and children, which occasion different pleasures and pains, which are kept private, as belonging to private persons. But being of one opinion concerning their home, and all of them pointing towards the same end, as far as possible, to sharing one common feeling of pleasure and pain? Well, shall law-suits and accusations against one another be eliminated from among them, so to speak, by their possessing nothing themselves as private property but their bodies, and everything else being held in common, whereby they shall be liberated from all those disturbances which men raise about money, children and relations?' 'They shall be freed from all these difficulties.'

'Neither can there be any reason among them for any actions leading to violence or unseemly treatment. For, making the protection of their person a necessary duty, we will make it beneficial and just for those of equal age to help one another. Also, the elder shall be encouraged both to govern and admonish the younger. And the younger, as becomes them, shall never attempt to harm the elder, or in any way to be violent towards him. Nor will they, in any way, dishonour them, for there are sufficient Guardians to hinder that, both by fear of punishment and reverence for each other. Reverence on the one hand, restraining them from assaulting their parents, and fear of punishment in the case of harming sons, brothers, and fathers.

'In every respect, as far as it relates to the laws, the men and women shall all live peaceably with one another. And while they have no rebellion among themselves, there is no danger of any other city raising a disturbance against them, or that they will split into factions. As for the many lesser evils, from which they will be freed, I refer to that corrupting flattery of the rich. And either indigence or indulgence in the education of their children, and the need to procure money for the necessary support of their family, which is the problem of the poor. Sometimes having to borrow, and sometimes being despised, and sometimes using all manner of deceit, in procuring provisions, which they give to the use of their wives and domestics. How many slavish and mean sufferings, my friend, they endure in all these respects, are not even worthy to be mentioned.

'They will be delivered from all these anxieties, and will live more blessedly than that most blessed life, which even those live who gain the first prize in the Olympic Games! They are esteemed, and happy, on account of the small part of what these victors enjoy; for the victory of these men is nobler, and their maintenance by the public is more complete. As the victory they gain is the safety of the whole city, and both they and their children are crowned with all the necessities of life, and even laurels. They receive honour from their city while alive, and at their death an honourable funeral. The noblest of rewards! Do you remember that in our former reasoning, I do not know who it was objected to us, that we were not making our Guardians happy enough, who, though they had it in their power to have the whole wealth of their citizens, had nevertheless nothing at all? And we proposed to consider this afterwards, if it fell our way, but that at the present time we were making our Guardians only Guardians, and the city itself as happy as possible, but without regarding one particular class in it, with a view to make them the happiest.

'What do you think now of the life of our auxiliaries, which seems to be far nobler and happier, than that of those who gain the prize at the Olympic Games? It does not at all appear to resemble the life of the leather-cutter, the handi-craftsman, or farmer. However, it is proper that I mention here what I once said on a former occasion, that if the Guardians shall attempt to be happy in such a way as to be no longer good Guardians, nor be content with this moderate, and steady best way of life; but being seized with foolish and youthful opinions about happiness, and shall, because they have it in their power, be driven to make themselves masters of every thing in the city, they shall know that Hesiod was truly wise in saying that the half is somehow not more than the whole.'

'If they take me,' Adimantus said, 'for their counsellor, they will remain in such a life, happy as Guardians.' 'You permit,' I asked, 'that the women act in common with the men, as we have explained, with respect to education and the breeding of children, and the Guardianship of the other citizens, both in remaining in the city, and in going forth to war. And that along with the men they ought to keep guard, and in every case to take a share in all arrangements as far as they can, and that while they perform these services they will do what is best, and act in no way contrary to the nature of the female sex with respect to the male sex, by which nature they are made to act one with another. Does not this,' I said, 'remain to be discussed, whether it is possible that this community can take place among men and women, in the same way as among other animals? And how far is it possible?'

'You have prevented me,' he said, 'in mentioning what I wished to ask. For, in relation to warlike affairs, how will they fight?' 'They will jointly embark on military expeditions, and will carry along with them such of their children as are grown up, so that, like those other pupils, they may see what it will be necessary for them to practise in battle when they are grown up. And besides seeing, that they may serve and take part in everything appertaining to war, and assist both their fathers and mothers in battle. Or, have you not observed what happens in the crafts? When, for instance, the children of the potters, serving their parents for a long time, look on, before they apply themselves to making earthenware?' 'Yes, indeed, and are our Guardians able to instruct their children with greater care, by that practice, and seeing what belongs to their office?' 'To suppose those children, could take greater care than our Guardians, is ridiculous, but every creature will fight better in the presence of their offspring.'

'But is there a danger, Socrates, when they are defeated, as is often the case in war, that when their children, as well as themselves, are cut off, it shall be impossible to build another city.' 'True,' I replied, 'but do you imagine we should, first of all, take care never to run any risk?' 'By no means.' 'What then, if they are all to risk themselves, is it not then, if they succeed, they shall become better men?' 'That is obvious, but do you imagine it is a small matter, and not worthy of the risk, when children, who are destined to be military men, see affairs relating to war, or not?' 'No, it is a matter of some consequence with regard to that. We must first endeavour to make our children spectators of the war, but contrive for them a place of safety, and then it shall be well, will it not?

'And shall not our parents, in the first place, being men, not be ignorant, but understand which of the campaigns are, and which are not dangerous? That they shall bring them into the safe campaigns, but with respect to the others they will be on their guard. And they will probably set Governors over them, not those that are the most depraved, but such as by experience and years are able leaders and attendants. But we will say that many things happen contrary to expectation. With reference to such events as these, it is proper that while they are children they sprout wings, as it were, so that, in any necessity, they may escape by flight. They must, when very young, be mounted on horses, and taught to ride on horseback, and brought to see the battle, not on high-mettled and warlike horses, but on the fleetest, and those that are most obedient to the reins. So that they shall, in the best manner, observe the work, and, in necessity, shall escape with the greatest safety, following their elder leaders.

'But what,' I said, 'as to the affairs of war? How are you to manage your soldiers, both with respect to one another and their enemies? That whoever of them leaves his rank, throws away his arms, or does any such act from cowardice, he must be demoted to the class of a handicraftsman, or land-labourer? And shall not the man who is taken prisoner, be given freely to any who inclines to employ him in the country, just as they please? And are you of the opinion, that he who gains in character, and excels, ought, in the first place, during the expedition itself, be crowned in some fashion, by every one of the youths and boys who are his fellow soldiers? Or do you think otherwise?' 'I am of the opinion, for my part, that they ought to be crowned, and be congratulated by everyone. And I will add to this law, that while they are upon this expedition no one shall be allowed to refuse them, whoever they are inclined to embrace, as if any happen to fall in love with anyone else, either male or female, he will be keener to win the prizes.'

'Very well,' I said, 'for we have already agreed that there are more sexual liaisons provided for the very best citizens, and a more frequent choice in such matters is allowed them than the others, so that the descendants of such noble ones may be as numerous as possible. But surely, even according to Homer's opinion, it is just that noble youth who are brave and should be honoured in this way. For Homer says that Ajax, who excelled in war, was rewarded with a large share of delight, at the entertainments, this being the most natural reward for a brave man in the bloom of youth, by which he, at the same time, acquires honour and strength. We shall then obey Homer, at least, in these affairs. And we shall honour the good, both at our sacrifices, and on all such occasions, in as far as they appear to be deserving, with hymns, and with those sexual joys we lately mentioned, and besides these treats, with special seats, and silver dishes, and full goblets, so that at the same time we may both honour and exercise the virtue of worthy men and women.

'And, if any one of those who die in the army shall have distinguished himself, shall we not, in the first place, say that he is of the golden race? And we shall believe Hesiod, when telling us, that when any of these die, "Good, holy, earthly dæmons, they become, expelling evils, the true Guardians of mankind". And we shall ask the oracle in what manner we ought to bury dæmoniacal and divine men, and with what marks of distinction, and so we will bury them in that very manner which the oracle decrees. And we shall in later times reverence and worship their tombs as those of dæmons. And we shall enact by law, that the same rites be performed, and in the same manner, to any man or woman, who shall have been known to have remarkably distinguished themselves in life, when they die of old age, or anything else?

'But what now? How shall our soldiers behave towards enemies? First, as to bringing enemies into slavery. Do you think it is just that Greeks should enslave Greek citizens? Or rather, as far as they are able, not permit any others to do it, and accustom themselves to this custom, to be sparing of the Grecian race, and being greatly on their guard against being enslaved by the Barbarians? It is, in general, and in every particular case, best to be sparing. They are not to acquire any Grecian slave themselves, and to counsel the other Greeks to act in the same manner. They will be the better, and by such conduct, turn themselves against the Barbarians, and abstain from enslaving one another.

'Also, they are not to strip the dead,' I said, 'of anything but their arms after they conquer them. It gives an excuse to cowards not to move against the enemy who are alive, as not being allowed to be pillaging anyone who is dead, as many armies have been lost by this plundering. And does it not appear to you to be illiberal and sordid, and the part of an effeminate and petty mind, to strip the dead body, and disrespect the body of the deceased enemy, when the enemy has fled, and there is only left behind the weapons with which he bravely fought? Or, do you imagine that those who act in this manner are in any way different from dogs, which bark in rage at the stones which are thrown at them, not touching the man who throws them? We must forego this stripping of the dead, and those hindrances arising from the carrying off of booty.

'Nor shall we at any time bring arms into the temples, as

if we were to dedicate them, certainly not the arms of Grecians, if we have any concern to obtain the good will of the other Greeks, but we shall also be afraid, that it should be a profanation to bring into the temple such belongings as these, from our own kinsmen; unless, of course, the oracle shall decree otherwise.' 'That is most correct,' he replied. 'But what about laying waste to Grecian lands, and the burning of their houses. How shall our soldiers behave towards their enemies?' 'In my opinion, neither of these scourges should be executed, but only a year's produce be carried off. It seems to me, that just as these two words, war and sedition, are different, so there are two different customs which are signified by them. I call them two different customs, because the one is domestic and familiar, the other is foreign and strange. When hatred is felt between ourselves, it is called sedition; when it is against foreigners, it is called war.

'But consider now, if I make this point reasonably, for I affirm that the Greek nation is friendly, and allied to its own people, but is foreign and unfriendly to the Barbarian. When the Greeks fight with the Barbarians, and the Barbarians with the Greeks, we shall say that they wage war, and are natural enemies, and this hatred is to be called war. But when Greeks fight with fellow Greeks, we shall say that they are friends by nature, and that Greece in such a case is distempered, and in rebellion, and such a conflict is to be called sedition. Consider,' said I, 'that in the sedition previously mentioned, wherever such a laceration happens, and the city is disjointed, if they sequester the lands, and burn the houses of one another, how destructive the rebellion becomes, and neither of them seem to be true patriots. Otherwise they would never dare to lay waste the land of their mother country; but it would satisfy the victors to carry off the fruits of the vanquished, and to consider how they are to be reconciled, and not be perpetually at war.

'But what now?' I said. 'Is not this city we are establishing to be a Greek one? And shall not the citizens be good and mild? And shall they not be lovers of their fellow Greeks? And shall they not account Greece as familiar to them? And shall they not have the same religious rites as the rest of the Greeks? A difference then with Greeks, is as with kinsmen, they will call a sedition, a sedition, and not a war. And they will behave towards them as those who are to be reconciled. They should then be mild and moderate, not punishing for the sake of punishing, so far as to enslave or destroy, since they are moderate people, and not inwardly hostile. Neither, as they are Greeks, should they sequester Grecian lands, nor burn their houses, nor will they act as if in every city all are their enemies, men, women, and children. But that only a few are their enemies, the real authors of the quarrel. So on all these accounts they will neither choose to lay waste lands, as the greatest number of their opponents are their friends, nor will they overturn their houses, but will carry on the war so far, until the guilty be obliged to make peace with the innocent, whom they distressed. And they shall make due reparation.' 'I agree,' he said, 'that we should behave in this way towards our fellow citizens when we are set one against another, and not to behave towards the Greeks as presently the Barbarians do to one another. Let us establish this law for our Guardians, neither to lay waste the lands, nor burn the houses.' 'Let us establish it once and for all.'

'Now Socrates,' said Glauco, 'please tell us how far such an ideal government is actually possible? For, if it be at all possible, I will allow that all these good principles should belong to that city, and that they will, in the best manner, fight against their enemies, and follow all your other rules, and never abandon one another, recognizing their kinship, and calling one another by these names, such as father, son, and brother; and if the women shall camp along with them, whether in the same rank, or drawn up behind them, that they will also strike terror into their enemies, and at the same time assist the men, if ever there be necessity for it. I know that in this way we will entirely be invincible. And I clearly see too what advantages they have at home. But I shall speak no more about this government, as I allow that all these matters, and ten thousand other things, will belong to it, if it can actually exist. But let us endeavour to persuade one another of this question, whether it actually is possible, and in what respect it is so, and let us put on one side those other questions you may have omitted.'

'You have suddenly,' I replied, 'made an assault on my reasoning, and make no allowance for a rational loiterer, such as myself, for perhaps you do not remember that with some difficulty, I escaped from two tidal waves, and now you are throwing upon me the greatest and most dangerous of the three. You must entirely forgive me, that with good reason I avoided, and was afraid to mention so great a paradox, and failed to undertake to examine it.' 'The more,' he said, 'you fail to mention these things, the less will you be freed from explaining to what degree this government is possible or not. Proceed please, and do not delay!' 'Must not it, in the first place, be remembered,' I said, 'that we have come here in search of the meaning of justice, what it is, and what injustice is?' 'We must,' he said, 'but how is this relevant to our purpose of finding out whether such a republic is actually possible?'

'Dear friend, if we discover what justice truly is, we shall see that the just man should, in no respect, be different from justice itself, and in every way aim to be just as justice is? And shall we not be satisfied if we approach as near to it as possible, so that all others can partake of it too? I repeat, that we are enquiring into what actually justice is, and we are also in quest of the just man, and are considering what kind of man he should be, if he does exist. We likewise enquired into what injustice is, and who are the most unjust men, in order that, investigating into these two models, and what kind of men they appear to be, with regard to happiness and its opposite. We might then be obliged to acknowledge, concerning ourselves, whoever most resembles them in character; and not only for this end, just to show whether such a State is possible or not.

'Do you imagine that the painter is in any degree less excellent, who having painted a model of a most handsome man, and brought everything fully into his picture, is yet unable to show that such a man really exists?' I said. 'Well then, have we not made clear in our reasoning what is an exact model of an ideally Good city? Have we said anything for the worse, do you think, on this account, that we are not able to show, whether it is possible or not, for an ideal city to be established such as we have described? This then, is the truth of the matter. But if now, on your account, I must show how, especially, and in what respects, whether it is possible or not; in order to make this discovery, you must again accept the same propositions as before. Firstly, is it actually possible for any plan to be executed so perfectly as it is described? Or, is it the nature of practice, that it never approaches so near the truth as theory, though some may think otherwise? So will you allow this or not?' 'I allow it,' he said.

'Do not then oblige me to show you again all these details, in every respect, so perfectly as we have described it in our reasoning already. But if we are able to find out how a city may be established, as near as possible to what we have reasoned, you may say, that we have then discovered that these ideals, which we enquire about, are possible. We are now, it seems, at the next stage, to endeavour to find that out, and to show what is the evil which is now infecting cities, when they are not established in the manner we have described. And what is the smallest change possible, which, if made, would bring a city into line with this model of government. So let us see if this can be effected preferably by the change of one factor, if not by the change of two, if not that, by the change of the fewest factors in number, and the smallest in power.

'By the change of one factor,' I said, 'I am able, I believe, to show that the State can fall into this model of government. But the change is not indeed small or easy, yet it is possible. I am now coming to what I compared to the greatest ocean wave, and it shall now be mentioned, though, like a breaking wave, it might overwhelm us with excessive laughter and unbelief. But consider what I am going to say. Unless, either true philosophers actually govern and guard our cities, or those who, at present are called Kings and Governors, philosophize genuinely and sufficiently, then these two, the political power and philosophy, will not unite as one. And until the bulk of those, who at present pursue each of these functions separately, are of necessity excluded, there shall be no end, friend Glauco, to the miseries of cities, nor yet, as I imagine, to those of the human race! Not until then shall this polity, which we have gone over in our reasoning, will spring up to be a possibility, and behold the light of the sun.

'And here it seems to me to be necessary, if we are anyhow to make our escape from those evils we mentioned, accurately to define what kind of men these are, whom we call true philosophers, when we dare to assert that they alone should govern. In order that, when this is made perfectly clear, anyone may be able to defend himself, when he asserts that to those men or women, the right naturally belongs, both to apply themselves to philosophy, and likewise to take upon themselves the government of the State. But all the others are not to apply themselves either to philosophy or government, but to obey their ruler.' 'It is proper,' he said, 'to define these principles.' 'Come then, follow me this way, and let us see if together we can sufficiently answer this question.

'Will it be necessary,' I said, 'to remind you, or do you remember it, when we say of anyone, that if he loves anything, when we speak with propriety, he must not appear to love one part of it, and not another, but to have an affection for the whole. Shall we not similarly say that the philosopher is desirous of wisdom, and not of one part only, but of the whole? He who is opposed to learning, especially if he is young, and has not at all the understanding to discern what is the Good, and what is otherwise, shall not be called a lover of learning, nor a philosopher! But the man who readily inclines to imbibe every mode of learning, and with pleasure, enters on the study of it, and is insatiable for it, that man we shall with justice call a philosopher, shall we not?' On this point Glauco said, 'There will be many such philosophers, and many may be quite absurd, for all your lovers of ostentation appear to me to be of this kind, just taking pleasure in learning, to show off. And your sound so-called lovers of learning, are the most strange of all, to be reckoned with, among pseudo philosophers. I mean those who would not willingly attend to such reasoning, and such a discourse as this, but yet, as if they hire out their ears to listen to every chorus, they run about to the nearest Bacchanalia, omitting no cities or villages. Shall all these, and others, studious in such matters, and those who apply themselves to the inferior arts, be called by us philosophers?'

'By no means,' I said, 'they only resemble true philosophers.' 'But whom,' he said, 'do you call the true ones?' 'Those,' I said, 'who are desirous of discerning the truth!' 'This,' he said, 'is right. But what exactly do you mean by the truth?' 'It is not easy,' I said, 'to explain it to another, but you, I imagine, will agree with me in this respect, that since the beautiful is opposite to the deformed, these are two different qualities. And if they are two, then each of them is one. And the reasoning is the same concerning justice and injustice, good and evil. And concerning every other matter, the argument is the same, that each of them is one in itself, but appears to be many, being everywhere diversified by their communication with action and body, and with one another. In this manner then, I separate these two, and set apart those you have mentioned, the lovers of public shows, of handicrafts, and mechanics and so forth on the one hand. And apart from these, on the other hand, I set those of whom we discourse with at present, whom alone we may properly call aspiring philosophers.

'The lovers of spectacles delight in fine sounds, colours, processions, and every bizarre spectacle which makes up these Bacchanalia, but as for the real nature of beauty and truth itself, their minds are unable to discern and admire. But as to those who are able to approach beauty and truth, and to behold them as they are in themselves, are they not few in number? He who casually calls some things beautiful and others true, but does not really know beauty and truth itself, and is unable to follow, even if one were to lead him by the nose, to the knowledge of it, doesn't he seem to you to live in a dream, or is he awake? Consider now, what is it to dream? Is it not this, when a man, whether asleep or awake, imagines the similitude of a thing is not actually the real similitude, but only something which it resembles? But what about he who judges in the opposite way to this, who understands what beauty and truth are in themselves, and is able to discern both it, and such qualities that participate in it, but does not think the participants themselves to be the whole of beauty or truth, nor the whole of beauty and truth to be the participants? Does such a person seem to you to be awake, or in a dream?' 'Awake,' he said.

'May we not then properly call this man's mental perception philosophical, as he really understands what true knowledge is, but of the other, a sham philosopher, who only offers opinions? Shall we decide correctly by calling them "lovers of opinion", rather than philosophers?' 'And yet they will be greatly enraged at us if we call them so.' 'Not if they be persuaded by me, for it is not seemly to be enraged by the truth. Those who admire every thing which has real being, are to be called true philosophers, and not mere lovers of opinion.

BOOK 6

ROLE OF THE GUARDIAN

'What then,' he said, 'are we to investigate next?' 'What else,' I said, 'but that which is next in order? Since those are philosophers who are able to meet up with that which always exists unchangeably, and recognize the principle of immutably. But those who are not able to accomplish this, but who wander about with their minds flitting from branch to branch between many things, are continuously shifting from one idea to another, are not genuine philosophers. Which of these two should best be suited to be the Governors of the city?' 'Which way, shall we determine this, and determine it reasonably?' he asked. 'Whichever of them,' I replied 'that appears capable of preserving the laws and institutions of the city; these are to be made the Guardians.

'Consider then, that they be empty of falsehood, not willing at any time to tell a lie, and hate deception, and love the truth. Can you find any quality more allied to wisdom than truth? Is it possible that the same mind can be philosophic, and at the same time be a lover of falsehood? He, who is in reality a lover of learning, should immediately, from his infancy, be in the greatest degree desiring to find out the truth. And whosoever has such a strong inclination to pursue learning, and every ideal of this kind, would be conversant, I think, with the refined pleasures of the soul itself, and would forsake those gross pleasures which arise from the body, provided he is not a counterfeit, but a real philosopher. This follows on from a mighty need to know the truth. Such a one is moderate in his desires, and is by no means a lover of money, for the vain, selfish reasons why money is, with so much trouble, anxiously sought after.

'And surely you must similarly consider this, when you are to judge who has a philosophic mind, and who has not, so that your judgement, does not without your knowledge take an illiberal turn; for pettiness is opposed to a soul which is prepared to pursue earnestly the "all and everything", of that which is divine and true gnosis. Do you suppose that he who has magnificent conceptions in his mind, and the ability to contemplate the whole of time, and the whole of being, can possibly consider human life as of little consequence? Such a person will not consider death to be anything awesome either. A cowardly and illiberal mind will not, in my opinion, readily participate in true philosophy.

'Well now, can the moderate man, and one who is not a lover of money, nor illiberal, nor arrogant, nor cowardly, ever possibly be an unjust co-partner in the philosophical pursuit? And you will likewise consider what constitutes the philosophic soul, and what does not; whether it is just and mild, or antisocial and savage. Nor, I think, will you omit this ability, as to whether he learns with facility or with difficulty. Here are some pertinent questions for you to consider. What if he can retain little of what he learns, being quite forgetful, is it possible for him to be a philosopher? And when he labours unprofitably, do you not imagine he will be at last obliged to hate both himself and such practice? We should never count a forgetful soul among those who are to become thoroughly philosophic, but we shall require him or her to have a good memory.

'And we shall say this at least, that an unmusical and lewd nature leads anywhere else but towards sound, good judgement. But, do you reckon truth is allied to the Good? Let us require among other qualities, a mind that is naturally well-proportioned and graceful, as a proper guide towards spontaneously attaining the essence of each quality that we term Beingness. Well, do we not in some measure seem to you to have discussed the necessary qualifications to be a philosopher, and such qualities as are consequent, one with the other, in a soul that is to apprehend Beingness sufficiently, and to perfection?

'Is it possible for you, in any measure, to blame such a study as this, when a man is unable sufficiently to apply himself to learning, unless he has a good memory, learns with facility, is magnanimous, graceful, and is the friend and ally of truth, justice, fortitude and temperance! Now, I think, everyone will allow us, that such a man or woman, with all those qualifications we have listed, is one who is qualified to be a sound philosopher. Such a man or woman rarely arises among mankind, and there are very few of them, don't you think? If these qualities constitute philosophic genius, which we have established meets with suitable instruction, he or she will, I believe, necessarily grow up to attain every virtue. But if, when sown in improper soil, he or she will grow up and be nourished weakly, accordingly, the philosophic quest will, on the other hand, turn into the opposite, unless the Gods grant the soul their assistance.

'Or do you think that certain of the youth are so corrupted by the sophists that they will fail to become good philosophers. These corruptors of youth are certain private sophists?

I say that each of these hirelings, which men call sophists, and whom I believe to be the rivals of the philosophic art, teach nothing else but dogmas of the vulgar, which they approve when they are assembled together, and call it the Good. When he is such a one, does he not, in heaven's name, appear to you to be an absurd teacher? For, if anyone converses with these men, and shows them either a poem, or any other production of fine art, or rule of administration respecting the city; and then makes the multitude the judges of that, he is under an overmastering necessity of doing whatever the vulgar commend. And in order to show that these works of art are in reality good and beautiful, have you at any time heard any of them advance a reason that was not quite ridiculous?

'When you attend to all these matters, bear this in mind, that the multitude never will admit or accept that there is the One Beautiful in itself, and not many beautifuls. I mean one thing itself which has a single subsistence, and not many such things. It is impossible for the multitude to become philosophers. And those who philosophize genuinely, are often reproached by them, and also by those sophisticated private persons, who, in conversing with the multitude, desire only to please them. From this state of affairs, what safety do you see for the philosophic genius to continue in his or her pursuit, and arrive at perfection?

'And consider from what was formerly said, for we have allowed those facilities in learning, memory, fortitude, and magnanimity to belong to this genius. And shall not such a one, of all men, immediately be the first even in boyhood; especially if he or she has a body naturally adapted to his or her soul, to move swiftly towards becoming a philosopher? And when he or she becomes more advanced in age, his or her kindred and citizens, I think, will wish to employ him or her in their affairs. And making supplications to him or her, and paying him or her homage, they will submit to him or her, and anticipate and flatter beforehand his or her growing powers.

'Now,' I said, 'what do you think that such a one will do, in such a case, especially if he or she happen to belong to a great city, and is rich, and of noble descent, handsome, and of an imposing stature? Will he or she not be filled with extravagant hopes, believing himself or herself capable of managing both the affairs of the Greeks and Barbarians, and on this account, carry him or herself loftily, without any solid judgement, full of ostentation and vain conceit? If one should gently approach a man of this disposition, and tell him the truth, that he has no judgement, yet needs it; and furthermore that it is not to be acquired by one who subjects himself to this arrogance; do you think that, with all these evils about him, he will be ready to listen? If now,' I said, 'through a good natural disposition, and an innate tendency to reason, anyone could somehow be made sensible, and be bent and drawn towards philosophy.

'But what do we imagine those others will do, when they reckon they will lose his company, and the benefit which they previously received from him? Will they not by every action, and every speech, say and do everything to the man to persuade him otherwise; and as to his mentor, to render him incapable, by ensnaring him in private, and possibly bringing him to public trial? Is it possible now that such a one will philosophize? You see,' I said, 'that we were right when we affirmed that even the very qualities of the philosophic genius, when they meet with bad education, in some measure may fall from this pursuit. Such then, admirable friend, is the ruin, and great corruption of the best aspirants for this noblest pursuit, which rarely happens, as we observed.

'And from among these sophists, are the men who commit the greatest mischief in cities, and to private persons; and in contrast, they who do the greatest good, are those who happen to be drawn to the side of true philosophy. But impoverished souls never did anything remarkable for anyone, either to a private person or to a city. Those, whose vocation is chiefly to apply themselves to philosophy, have often fallen away, leaving Goddess Athene desolate. Such impoverished souls lead themselves a sad life, neither becoming wise nor authentic. Also, many other unworthy persons intrude on philosophy, then abandoning that study in an ungrateful manner, they have disgraced her, and attacked her with reproaches. They claim that those who converse with the philosophic muse are of no value, and most of them deserve punishment.

'And with good reason are they said, for other contemptible men seeing the field unoccupied, like persons who have made an escape from prisons to temples; these rogues gladly leap from their handicrafts to philosophy as a livelihood. But, even in this situation of philosophy, her remaining dignity, in comparison with all the other arts, still surpasses them all in magnificence; a dignity many wish to possess, who by natural disposition are unfit for it, and whose bodies are not only deformed by their arts and handicrafts, but whose souls also, are in like manner confused, and crushed by their servile works. Does it seem to you,' I said, 'that they are not in any way different in appearance from the village blacksmith who has made a little money, bald and puny, recently liberated from chains, only recently washed in the bath, with a new robe on him, decked out as a bridegroom, presuming to marry the daughter of his master, encouraged by the poverty and forlorn circumstances with which he sees her oppressed?'

'I can see, now Socrates, why you are famed for your wit and sardonic irony, but seriously, there is no great difference between them and the local smithy.' 'What sort of a race must men such as these produce? Must it not be bastardly and abject? Well, when men who are unworthy of instruction apply themselves to it, and are conversant with it, in an unworthy manner, what kind of sentiments and opinions are produced? Are they not men who should properly be called sophists, and who possess nothing genuine, or worthy of true judgement?

'A very small number of us now remain. Adimantus is one of those who are worthily conversant in philosophy, while the rest happen either to be detained somewhere in banishment or are learning with us, and whose generous and well-cultivated disposition persists in the study of philosophy, having been removed from everything which tends to corrupt it. Or else when, in a small city, some mighty soul arises, who despising the honours of the State, the State entirely neglects him. And similarly some small number might come to philosophy from other callings, which they justly despise, being of a noble nature. And even from these few, such as are tasting, and have tasted, how sweet and blessed the acquisition of philosophy is, and have sufficiently seen the madness of the multitude, and how none of the vulgar effects anything salutary in the affairs of cities. And he sees that there is no ally, who might go to the assistance of the just, and be safe, and that he is like one falling among wild beasts. He is neither willing to join them in injustice, nor able, as he is but only one alone, to oppose the whole savage crew.

'And, before he can benefit the city or his friends, he is destroyed, and is unprofitable both to himself and to others; just alone reasoning on all these things, keeping quiet, and attending to his own affairs, as in a tempest, when the dust is driven, and the sea agitated by winds. He is like a man standing under a wall, watching others overwhelmed in iniquity; he is satisfied if he shall pass his life here, free from injustice and unholy deeds, and make his exit in due course, in good hopes, keeping cheerful and benign.' 'And before he shall make his exit,' he said, 'he may have achieved something that is considered to be more than a trifle. But be careful Socrates, if they hear you say such things as that, they will be after you, on some trumped-up charge or other.'

I continued after that interjection, 'Yes, dear boy, while the true philosopher has not met with a city that is suitable for him to live in, then in a suitable place, he shall try to make a greater use of himself, and shall preserve his rights as a private person as well as those of the public as a whole. But at present, those who engage in this divine work are striplings, who immediately from childhood, before they come to their domestic affairs and mercenary employments, apply themselves to the most abstruse parts of philosophy, and then leave it because it is beyond them. And yet, they are held to be most consummate philosophers by some. I call the most difficult part of philosophy to be that of respecting the art of pure reasoning and sound logic. And, after some time, when they are invited by others who practise this true art, they are pleased to become hearers, and think it a great condescension, reckoning they ought to do it as a hobby. But when they approach old age, full of regrets for wasting their lives, with a few exceptions, they are extinguished much more quickly than even the Heraclitean sun, because they are never again rekindled.'

'But how should they act?' he asked. 'Quite the reverse. While they are boys they should apply themselves to juvenile instruction in philosophy, while taking proper care of their bodies, through gymnastics, so they shoot up and grow to firmness, thus providing for philosophy some proper service. Then, as their age advances, in which the soul begins to be perfected, they should vigorously apply themselves to their exercises; and when strength eventually decays, and is no longer suitable for civil and military service, they should then be dismissed, and retire at leisure, and, except as an occupation, to do nothing else but contemplate divine philosophy, if they wish to live happily. Then, when they die, to possess in the next world a destiny adapted to the life they have led in this one.

'But as for the man who has arrived at the model of virtue, and has been moulded similar to it in the most perfect manner possible, both in word and in deed, many have never at any time seen such a man, neither one nor more of that kind. Nor yet, my dear Glauco, have they sufficiently listened to beautiful and liberal reasoning, so as to ardently investigate the truth, by every means, for the sake of knowing it well. They should keep at a distance any intricate and contentious debates, which tend to nothing else but to opinion and strife, both in the courts of justice and in private meetings. On these accounts then, and foreseeing these events, we used to be afraid.

'However, being compelled by the truth, we now assert, that neither city nor polity, nor even a man, in the same way, would ever become perfect, until some necessity of fortune obliged these few philosophers, who are at present not depraved or useless, to take the government of the city in their hands, and compel the city to be obedient to them. Or else wait until the sons of those who now hold the offices of power and magistracies, or they themselves, by some divine inspiration, be possessed with a genuine love of true philosophy. Moreover I affirm that no one has reason to think that either of these, or both are impossible, otherwise we might justly be laughed at for making statements which are otherwise only similar to pious prayers.

'So, in the infinite series of past ages, the greatest necessity has obliged men that have arrived at the summit of philosophy, sometimes to take on the government of a State. For somehow, Glauco, the man at least who really applies his mind to true Beingness, has not the leisure to step down to the petty affairs of mankind, and, in fighting with them, to be opposed with envy and ill nature. But, rather beholding and contemplating such objects as are orderly, and always existing in the same condition, such as neither to injure nor be injured by each other; but are in all respects beautiful, and according to reason, these he imitates and resembles as far as possible. The philosopher who converses with that which is decorous and divine, as far as is possible for man, becomes himself decorous and divine. And after this, don't you think they will draw a sketch of the ideal republic?

'Afterwards, I think, as they fill in their work, they will frequently look all ways, both to what is naturally just and beautiful, and temperate, and again to that which they are establishing among mankind. They will blend and compound their knowledge from different characters and pursuits, drawing from that which Homer calls the divine likeness, and the divine resemblance subsisting among men. They will, I think, strike out one error and insert another truth, until they have rendered human manners, as far as is possible, dear to the Gods. While their genius is like this, and meets with suitable exercise, it will become perfectly sound and philosophic. Will they still be enraged at us when we say that until the philosophic class orders the government of the city, neither the miseries of the city nor of the citizens shall have an end? And that this republic, which we now speak of in the way of a fable, will arrive in reality at perfection?

'Suppose that they are persuaded by this wisdom. Then is there anyone who will allege that those of philosophic genius cannot possibly spring from a line of kings and sovereigns?' 'Nobody,' he said, 'would ever allege that, and even if they were born with a philosophic genius, no one would say they are under a greater risk of being corrupted, although it is a difficult matter for these geniuses to be untainted, even we ourselves agree.' 'But,' I said, 'in the infinite cycle of time of the whole of the human race, there should arise some men or women who are pure and untainted. But surely, a single one is sufficient, if he exists, and has a city subject to him, to accomplish everything that is now so much disbelieved. And when that Governor, has established the laws and customs we have agreed upon, it is not at all impossible that the citizens would be most willing to obey him.

'But isn't it wonderful, and not impossible, that what seems to us to be true, should also seem to be true to others? And that this reasoning is the best, and that it is possible, as we have sufficiently explained in the earlier part of our discourse. Now it seems we have agreed upon our legislation and that the laws we mention are the best; but that it is difficult to establish them, but not impossible.

'Now we must even dare to assert this, that the most complete Guardians must be philosophers. But remember that you will probably have only a few of them. For such a genius, as we said, is seldom found in one man, but its different talents generally spring up in different persons. For such as are able to learn with facility, have a good memory, are sagacious and acute, and endued with whatever qualifications are allied to these, are not necessarily at the same time, vigorous and magnanimous in their minds, so as to live orderly, with quietness and stability. But, those that are governed by their acuteness and equanimity, wherever it happens, everything that is stable stays with them. With regard to these firm habits of the mind, which are always versatile, and are trustworthy, and are difficult to be removed, even by dangers of war, are of the same temperament with reference to learning. Surely, they must be tried in all respects we formerly mentioned, in labours, in challenges, and in pleasures. And similarly in what we then passed over, and are now mentioning, we must exercise them in various kinds of learning, whilst we consider whether their genius is capable or not of sustaining the greatest disciplines, or whether it will fail, as those who fail in other ways.' 'It is proper now,' he said, 'to consider this question in this manner. But what, Socrates, do you call the greatest disciplines?'

'You remember in some measure, that when we had distinguished that the soul contained three parts, we reasoned concerning justice, temperance, fortitude, and wisdom, and what each of them is. We somewhere said, that it was possible to perceive these qualities in their most beautiful forms, but that the journey would be tedious which we must take, but that it was possible, however, to approach towards them in the way we have demonstrated. And you said that this was sufficient. But in my opinion what was then advanced came far short of accuracy or being sufficient, so please answer my question.' 'To me, they seemed to be discussed in the correct manner, and the rest seemed to think so too.' 'But, friend, in speaking of serious matters of this kind, such a discourse that leaves out any part of the truth, is not altogether a complete discourse. So there are times when there is great necessity for further enquiry.

'To continue, very many, are affected by laziness. But the Guardian of the city, and its laws, has no room for that fault. Such a one, my friend, must make a more ample circuit around the topic, and work as much at study as in the exercises, otherwise, as we are now saying, he will never arrive at the perfection of this most important and auspicious learning.' 'But is there anything greater than justice, and those virtues which we have discussed?' he said. 'Yes, there is something much greater!' I said. 'And even with these questions we can only contemplate the crude description, but we must not omit making the best attempt. Isn't it ridiculous if in other matters of small account, we employ our whole effort, and strive to make them most accurate and perfect, yet not believe that the highest and most important question worthy of our highest attention is the pursuit of truth, in order to make ourselves more perfect?' 'That sentiment,' he said, 'is very just. But, do you really think, that anyone will leave you without asking, what indeed is this greatest discipline, and about what is it conversant with, when you call it so important?'

'Not at all, but do you yourself ask me? For assuredly you have often heard it, and at present you either do not attend, or you intend to give me trouble again, by expecting more of me. In fact, I think, that you have often heard that the idea of the Good is the greatest discipline, which idea, when justice and the other virtues support it, becomes the most useful and advantageous. You now almost know that this is what I mean to say, yet we do not sufficiently realize that idea. And if we do not understand it, then without this knowledge, although we may have understood everything else to the highest degree, we know that it is of no real advantage to us. In the same way it would be as good as nothing, if we possessed everything whatsoever, without possessing the knowledge of the Good! So do you really think there is any greater profit in possessing all things, without the possession of the Good, and in knowing all things without the knowledge of the Good, and still not experiencing anything at all that is both beautiful and the Good?

'But surely at least you know, that from the many pleasures available, only some seem to be the Good; and to the more refined, that seems to form intelligence. You know also, my friend, that they who think they know what intelligence is cannot explain what it really is. But if you press them, finally they will say it is intelligence that is the Good! How indeed can it be otherwise? If, when they upbraid us, that we do not know what is the Good, they speak to us as though we did know, and call it the intelligence to be what is the Good, as if we understood what they say when they pronounce the word Good. Well, are those who define pleasure to be the Good, less infected with error than the others? Or are these also obliged to confess that there are injurious pleasures?

'It happens, I think, that they acknowledge that the same thing can be both good and evil, do they not? Is it not evident, that there are great and manifold doubts about what is the Good? Again, is it not also self-evident, that with reference to anything we may term just and beautiful, many would choose the apparent, even though that is not really as it seems to be, and yet they think they possess an understanding of them? But the acquisition of knowledge, that is only apparent, never satisfied anyone. Yet they seek what is real, and here, everyone who knows the real, despises what is only the apparent.

'This is what every refined soul pursues; and for the sake of this, it does everything, professing that it is something to be achieved, but being dubious, and unable to comprehend sufficiently what it truly is; and in order to possess the same stable belief, respecting it just like other things. They then lose the advantage of the so-called other things, if there be in them any advantage. About such a topic of so mighty a consequence, shall we not agree, that even those, our very best men in the city, and to whom we commit the management of everything, are also in the dark? I think that while it is unknown in what way the just and beautiful are truly the Good, they will not have a Guardian of any great value, if he is ignorant of this great truth. And I prophesy that no one will arrive at the knowledge of truth, justice and beauty before he adequately knows what the Good really is.'

'You speak well, Socrates, now in the same way that you have spoken of justice and temperance, and other virtues, will you please discourse, concerning the Good?' 'And I too should be very well satisfied to do so, my friend, but I am afraid I shall not be able, for by appearing so readily disposed, I shall incur the ridicule of the unmannerly. No, friends, let us at present dismiss this enquiry, as to what the Good truly is, for it appears to me to be a subject that is too great for our present desire to get at just my own opinion.

But I am willing to tell you what the offspring of the Good seems to be, and what most resembles it, if this is agreeable to you, and if not, I shall dismiss it!' 'Do tell us, please Socrates, for you shall afterwards explain to us what the father of the offspring is, and that is the Good.' 'I wish both that I were able to give that explanation, and you will be able to receive it, and not as now, receive the offspring of it only.

'Receive now, then, this child and offspring of the Good itself. Yet take care however, that unwillingly I do not deceive you, in any respect, by giving an adulterated account of this offspring. I shall not tell you, until we have come to an agreement, and I have reminded you of what was mentioned in our preceding discourse, and has been frequently said on other occasions. Well, there are many things which are beautiful, and many which are good, and each of these we may say is so, and we distinguish them by our reasoning, and intellectual discrimination. But as to the Beautiful itself, and the Good itself, and in like manner concerning all those matters, now again we must bring these under one idea, as actually being One, and we shall assign to each that appellation which belongs to it. And those things, which are seen only by the eye, but are not objects of intellectual perception are not what we are seeking. For the true ideas are perceived by the intellect, and are not seen by the eye.

'By what part of ourselves do we see things that are visible?' 'By the sight.' 'Yes, and is it not by hearing that we perceive what is heard. But have you not observed,' I said, 'with regard to the Creator of the senses, how He has formed the power of sight, and of things being visible, in the most elaborate manner? Well, consider it in this way. Is there any other kind of faculty, which hearing and sound require, in order that the one may hear, and the other be heard, which third thing if it be not present, the one shall not hear, and the other not be heard?' 'There is nothing, and I imagine that neither do many others require any such other faculty; or can you mention anyone that does require it?' 'Oh, but with reference to the sense of seeing, and the object of sight, are you sure that you do not require something else?' 'What?'

'When there is sight in the eyes, and when he who has it attempts to use it, and when there is colour in the objects before him, unless there concurs some third kind of faculty, naturally formed for the purpose, you know that the sight will see nothing, and the colours will be invisible.' 'What is that you are speaking about?' 'Light!' I said. 'Then the bond which connects the sense of seeing, and the power of being seen, is by no small measure more precious than is the case with the other pairs, unless light is not more precious and present. Whom of the Gods in heaven, can you assign as the cause of this light, that makes our sight to see, and visible objects to be seen, in the best possible manner?' 'The same as you,' he replied, 'and others do, for it is evident that you mean the Sun.'

'Is not the sight then naturally formed in this manner with reference to this God? The sight is not the Sun, nor is that the Sun, in which sight is generated, which we call the eye. But I think that of all the organs of sense it is most like the solar form. And the power which the eye possesses is dispensed and flows from that solar power, which is within you? Is not the Sun, which indeed is not sight itself, yet is the cause of it, also seen by sight itself? Realize that this inner Light is what I call the offspring of the Good, which the Good generates, analogous to itself. And that what this is, in the region of intelligence, with respect to the intellect, and the objects of intellect, that the Sun is, in the region of the visible, with respect to sight and visible things, the offspring of the Good.

'You know that the eyes, when they are no longer directed towards objects whose colours are brought to them by the reflection of the light of the Sun, or by the luminaries of the night, grow dim, and appear almost nonexistent as if the eyes were lost. But when the eyes turn to objects which the Sun illuminates, then I think they see very clearly, and in those very eyes there appears now to be sight. Understand in the same manner, with reference to the soul. When it rests upon that which truth and real Beingness enlighten, then it understands and knows it, and appears to possess intelligence. But when it adheres to that which is blended with darkness, which is also generated, and which perishes or fades away, it is then conversant with mere opinion, its vision becoming blunted. So it wanders from one opinion to another, and resembles one without real intelligence or intellectual discrimination.

'That faculty, therefore, which imparts truth to what is known, and dispenses the power to him who knows, you may call the inner light which is an offspring of the Good, and is the cause of knowledge and of truth, and is best known through intelligence. And as both these two, knowledge and truth, are so beautiful, when you think that the Good is something different, and still even more beautiful than these, you shall think correctly. Knowledge and truth here are as light and sight there, which we rightly judged to be reflected from our own inner solar-form or that inward light, which is the offspring of the Good, but we are not to think it is just from the Sun alone. So here it is right to judge, that both these partake of the form of the Good; but to suppose that either of them is actually the Good, is not correct, for the Good itself is worthy of still greater honour.' 'You speak,' he said, 'of an inestimable beauty, since it creates knowledge and truth, but in itself is superior to these in beauty; for, I suppose that it is not exactly pleasure?'

'Hush!' I said, 'and in this manner consider its image still further. I think, that the Sun imparts to things which are seen, not only their visibility, but likewise their generation, growth and nourishment, not being itself the primary generation. We may say, therefore, that things which are known, not only derive this power from the Good, that they are known, but likewise that their Being and essence are also derived, while the Good itself is not essence, but actually beyond essence, transcending it both in magnificence and in power.' Here Glauco, with a very comical intonation, said, 'By Apollo this is a divine transcendence indeed!' 'You yourself,' I replied, 'are the cause, having obliged me to relate what appears to me the truth in respect of the Good.' 'And do not stop,' he said, 'but again discuss the allegory relating to the Sun, if you have omitted anything.' 'I think that much will be omitted, however, as far as I am able to show you at present, although I shall not willingly omit anything as the discourse progresses.

'Understand,' I said, 'that we say there are two lights. The one reigns over the intelligible and its place is inside you, here and now; and the other over the visible, like the Sun in the heavens. You understand there are these two categories, the visible and the intelligible? It is as if you would draw a line, cut it into two unequal parts, and then cut each section again, according to exactly the same ratio. Thus, other divisions of the visible category, and the intelligible category, when they are compared, one with the other, as to their perspicuity or clarity and obscurity or concealment, you will find that in the visible species you will have in one section several images. These images, in the first place, I call shadows, in the second place, reflections as in water, and such as subsist in bodies which are dense, polished and bright, and every thing of this kind, capable of mirroring, if you understand me?' 'I do, you have put the matter very perspicaciously, with the minimum of obscuration if I may so.' [laughter]

'Now, my witty friend, suppose we take the section which represents the visible, such as the animals around us, and every kind of plant, and whatever has a composite nature to be seen'. 'I am supposing it.' [More laughter] 'Please take this seriously, Glauco, it's not a joke! Then this section of visibility appears to be divided into true and untrue, and in the same proportion, which the object of opinion has to the object of knowledge. That is the very same proportion that the resemblance has, to that of which it is the resemblance? Now consider the section of the intelligible, how it should be divided? That with respect to one part of it, the soul uses the former sections as images; and is therefore obliged to investigate from hypotheses, not proceeding from the beginning, but to the conclusion. And the other part, the visible, is where the soul proceeds from that hypothesis to an unhypothetical principle, and without the help of those images, made by the intelligible themselves, works its way through them.' 'I have not,' he said, 'sufficiently understood you in these matters.' 'Well, we shall try again, for you will more easily understand me, when some further observations have cleared the way.

'For I think you are not ignorant of the fact that those who are conversant in geometry, and computations, after they have laid down hypotheses of the odd and even numbers and three kinds of angles, and other probabilities which are the sisters of these, reach abstract conclusions. Then, according to each method, they then proceed to examine these things as known, having first laid them down as hypotheses. They do not make any further reasoning about them, neither to themselves nor others, as now being propositions, which are obvious to all. So, beginning from these initial hypotheses, they directly discuss the rest, and with full consent, they end at the solution which their enquiry first pursued. And do you not similarly know, that when they take the visible evidence, and reason about it, their mind is not employed about these actual categories, but about those of which they are the resemblances, employing their reasoning about the square itself, and the diameter itself, and not about that which they actually draw?

'And, in the same manner, with reference to other particulars, those very things which they form and describe, in which category, shadows, and mirrored images in water, are to be reckoned. These they use as images, seeking to know those very things, which man can not otherwise see than by his mind. This is what I called the category of the intelligible. And I observed that the soul was obliged to use hypotheses in the investigation, not going back to look at the visible, as the images are not capable of ascending higher than the hypotheses. But we are making use of the images formed from things below, to lead to them above, into lucidity; which is usually esteemed to be distinct from the things themselves, and so highly valued.

'Understand now, that by the other section of the intelligible category, I mean that height which reason itself attains, making the hypotheses through its own reasoning power, not as principles, but really as hypotheses, like steps and handles. Thus, proceeding as far as to that which is unhypothetical, such as the fundamental principle of the universe, and coming into contact with it, again adhering to those things which adhere to the principle, it may thus descend to a conclusion. It does not utilize for this investigation anything which is sensible, but only abstract forms, proceeding through some, to others, and at length in forms terminating its progression. We want, however, clearly to state, that the perception of Real Being, and that which is intelligible, pursued by the science of reasoning, is more certain than the discoveries made by the sciences, as they are called, which have hypotheses as their first principles. And that those who perceive these are obliged to perceive them with their mind, and not with their inner sensibility, which comes from the soul. Thus, as they are not able to perceive, by ascending directly to the principle, but only from hypotheses, they appear to you, not to use the intellect in these researches, though they are of the intelligible category when taken in conjunction with the principle. You also appear to me to call the habit of geometrical and such like mathematics, the action of the intelligence, and not pure intellect; the intelligence subsisting somewhere between opinion and intellect.

'Well, Glauco, you have possibly comprehended sufficiently, and may conceive now, that corresponding to the four sections there are these four conditions in the soul: pure intellect answering to the highest and the first; the intelligence to the second; then assign faith to the third; and as to the fourth, conjecture. Arrange them likewise analogously, conceiving that they all participate in search of the truth, so that these all combine to create lucidity or clarity.'

BOOK 7

ALLEGORY OF THE CAVE

'After all these complex philosophical reasonings,' I said, 'let us now assimilate them with reference to education, and the want of education. Listen carefully, to the allegory I am about to give you, as it is highly significant and contains a great deal of metaphysical truth. Our nature, to such a condition as education, is as follows in this fable.

'Imagine several men who live in a subterranean habitation, like a cave, with its entrance opening up to the light, and shedding light on the whole extent of the cave. Imagine them to have lived in this cave since their childhood, with chains around their ankles and their necks, so as to stay there, and so they are only able to look in front of them, because of the chains, and they are incapable of turning their heads around.

Imagine them, also, to have the light of a great bonfire, blazing far above and behind them, and that from that fire, leading down towards those fettered men there is a straight road. Along this road, there is a low wall, built like those which fence the quack magicians, when they demonstrate their beguiling tricks on a stage. Imagine you now see, along this wall, men bearing all sorts of domestic utensils, raising them high above the wall. Along this wall one can see, by the firelight, statues of human beings, and different animals, sculpted in wood and stone, along with different kinds of furniture. And, some of those who are carrying these utensils are speaking, while others are silent.

'Now this allegorical fable resembles our human condition. In the first place, these chained men cannot actually see anything of themselves or of one another, but only the shadows formed by the fire, falling on the opposite wall of the cave? But what do you think they see of what is being carried along the wall? It is exactly the same. If they were able to talk with one another, don't you think they would consider it proper to give names to those very things which they saw before them? And what if the opposite part of this cave prison formed an echo, when any of those who passed along the wall spoke? Do you imagine they would deduce that this space was anything else than a place of passing shadows?

Such men as these will surely assume that there is nothing that can be called true, but the shadows of these utensils. Now with reference to both to their freedom from these chains, and their cure for their ignorance of what was actually passing, consider the nature of it, if such a thing should really happen to them. When anyone should be released from his chains, and obliged all of a sudden to rise up, and turn round his neck, and walk, then look up towards the light, then doing all these things, he would feel pained, and unable, because of the brightness of the light, to actually see the objects, of which he formerly saw as only shadows.

'Then what do you think he would say, if one should tell him that formerly he had seen only shadows, but now, being somewhat closer to reality, and turned around towards what was more real, he saw with more accuracy. And so, pointing out to him each of the objects which were passing along, we should question him, and oblige him to tell us what they were. Don't you think he would be both in doubt, and would believe that what he had formerly seen was more true than what was now being pointed out to him? And if we should oblige him to look into the light itself, wouldn't he feel pain in his eyes, because of the glare, and turning to such things as he is able to see close at hand, believe that these are clearly more real than those which are being pointed out?

'Now if one should drag him from the cave violently through a rough and steep ascent, and never stop until he drew himself up to the light of the Sun, would he not, while he was so drawn, be in torment, almost blinded, and be filled with rage? And after he had come to the light, having his eyes filled with glorious splendour, he would be unable to see any of these objects which were actually real. He would not be able to see them all of a sudden. But after some time he would become accustomed to the light and be able to see what was above him. First of all, he would most easily see shadows, afterwards the forms of men and what was reflected in the water, and after that the things themselves. And, with reference to these, he would more easily see the stars in the heavens, by looking by night at their light, and the moon, better than by day when looking at the light of the Sun. And, last of all, he may be able, I think, to perceive and contemplate the Sun himself, not reflected in water, but for himself by himself, in his own proper way.

'And after this amazing experience, he would now question himself, concerning who he actually was, conceiving that it was he, himself who has presented to his mind, the power of vision the seasons, the years, and that it was he who governed everything in that visible place. And he would conclude that of all those things which he formerly saw, he was the sole cause.

'Also when he remembers his first habitation in the cave, and the ignorance that was there, and those who were then his companions in chains, don't you think he will feel very happy by the change, and pity those who are still in fetters? And if there were there any honours and rewards to be awarded among themselves, for he who most acutely perceived what passed along the wall, and best remembered which of them passed first and which last, and which of them went together. And from these observations was able to forecast what was to happen. Doesn't it seem to you that he will desire such honours, and envy those who are already honoured, and empowered? Or, would he rather wish to suffer like Homer, and vehemently desire *As labourer to some ignoble man. To work for hire…and rather suffer anything than to possess such opinions, and live after such a manner*?

'But consider this further,' I said, 'if such a person should descend, and sit down again in the same place in the cave, wouldn't his eyes be filled with darkness, in consequence of coming down suddenly from the sunlight? And should he now again be asked to give his opinion of those shadows, and to argue about them with those who are still there eternally chained, while his eyes were still dazzled, and before they had recovered to their former state; and if this shouldn't happen in a short time, would he not make them laugh? And would it not be said of him, that, having ascended, he had returned with injured eyes, and that it was not proper even to attempt to go above, and that whoever should attempt to liberate them, and lead them up, if ever they were able to get him into their hands, they would put him to death?

'The whole of this allegory now, dear friend Glauco, is to be applied to our preceding discourse, and for what is to come. For, if you compare this region, which is seen by the sight, to be the habitation of the prison, and the light of the fire in it, to be the power of the Sun, then the ascent and vision of things above, leading to the soul's ascent into the region of the intelligible; you will apprehend my meaning, since you desired to hear it. But God only knows whether it is exactly true.

'Appearances present themselves to my understanding as follows. In the region of knowledge, the idea of the Good is the last object of vision, and is rarely to be seen. But if it is seen, we must conclude by reasoning that it is the cause of everything true, just and beautiful, generating in the visible sphere pure light from its lord the Sun. Furthermore in the intelligible place, the Good is itself the lord, generating truth, light and intellectual discrimination. This knowledge must be realized by him who is to act wisely, either in private or in public affairs.

'Come now,' I said, 'agree with me as well in this, and don't imagine that such as arrive at this understanding are unwilling to act in human affairs, although their souls always hasten to commune with the divine Goodness which dwells above, and inside us. It is somehow reasonable it should be so, if these experiences take place according to our previously mentioned allegory.

'Well then, don't you think that this is very wonderful, that when a man comes from divine contemplation on human evils, he should behave diffidently and appear somewhat awkward, whilst he is still dazzled. Especially if he is obliged, before he is sufficiently accustomed to the worldly darkness, to contend in the courts of justice, or elsewhere, about the shadows of justice, or those pillars which occasion the shadows; and to dispute about this point, when these revelations are not apprehended by those who have never at any time beheld real justice itself?

'But if a man possesses a sound intellect,' I said, 'he must remember, that there is a twofold disturbance of the visionary sight, arising from two causes; when we take ourselves from ethereal light to mundane darkness, and from mundane darkness to ethereal light. And when a man or woman considers that these very things happen with reference to the soul, whenever he sees anyone perplexed and unable to perceive anything, he will not laugh in a derisory manner, but will consider whether every soul is not coming from a more splendid life, to be darkened by ignorance, then going from dark ignorance to more luminous understanding, to be eventually filled with the dazzling splendour. So he will congratulate the fortunate soul on its destiny and life, and be compassionate towards the life and fate of the others who are not so fortunate. For if he wishes to laugh at the soul that grows from darkness to light, his laughter would be less improper, than if he were to laugh at the soul which descends from the light to darkness.

'It is right then,' I said, 'that we judge them in such a way as this, if these things be true. True education is not just as some that profess it and announce it to be. For they seem to say, that as there is no knowledge in the soul, they will insert it, as if they were inserting sight into blind eyes! But our present reasoning now shows that this power is inherent in the soul of everyone, and the organ by which everyone learns, and being in the same condition as the eye, if it were unable otherwise, than as with the whole mind and body, to turn from darkness to light; in like manner, the whole soul must be turned from the world of change, until it is able to endure the contemplation of Pure

Being. That is its own True Self, and the innermost divine splendour; and this we call the Good.

'This then,' I said, 'appears to be the important significance of this dialogue, in what manner we shall, with the greatest ease and advantage, be turned to enquire within. Not to implant in us the power of seeing which is already there, but considering ourselves as if we already possessed it, but only obscurely situated and looking at what method by which this may be accomplished. The other virtues of this soul, as it is called, seem to be somewhat resembling those of the body, for when they were not in it formerly, they are afterwards produced in it by good habits and right exercise. But that of wisdom happens to be of a nature much closer to the divine than any other virtue, as it never loses its power. But, according to the extent that the mind is inwardly turned, becomes useful and advantageous. If ignored it may become useless and even harmful.

'Or have you not observed, regarding those who are said to be wicked, yet cunning, how sharply their little soul can see, and how acutely it comprehends everything on which it is focused, and even compelled by the errant mind to be subservient to wickedness. However, if, from childhood, such a nature has been stripped of everything allied to the world of crude desires, which are like leaden weights around her, such trifles as riotous feastings, venereal excess and gluttony, then when repentantly turned inwards the mind leads the soul away from all these follies, the purified soul is freed. It will turn itself towards truth, and acutely see the Good, as it formerly saw the world.' 'It is most likely.'

'Again, isn't it also likely, and necessarily deduced from what has been said, that neither those who are uninstruct-ed and unacquainted with truth can ever sufficiently take good care of the city; nor those who just spend their whole time in learning useless facts about things which don't really matter, because they are unwilling to manage civil affairs? They think that while they are yet alive, they will migrate to the islands of the blest. What an illusion! Then it's our business to oblige those of the citizens who have the finest natures, to apply to their learning, what we said was of the greatest importance. That is, both to view the Good, and to ascend that ascent. And when they have so ascended, and sufficiently viewed the truth from there, we are not to allow them that which society now allows them.' 'What is that?' 'To continue there in solitude, and be unwilling to descend again to those wretched, fettered men, and alleviate their toils and suffering.'

'Are we acting unjustly towards them, and causing them to live a worse life, when they have it in their power to live a better one?' Glauco said. 'You have again forgotten, friend Glauco, that this is not the legislator's concern, in what manner any one class of men and women in the city shall live, but that he endeavours to affect the whole city, connecting the best citizens together by necessity and by persuasion, and making them share the advantages with one another by which they are able to benefit the whole community. And the legislator, when he creates such good men in the city, does it not mean that he may permit them to go where each may wish, but that, he himself may employ them for connecting the best elements of the city together?

'Consider, dear Glauco, that we shall in no way harm the philosophers who arise among us, but inform them about what is just, when we oblige them to take care of the others, and to serve as Guardians. We should allow that those who live in other cities also become philosophers. Every one eventually must, in turn, descend to the level of the others, and accustom himself to understand their obscure vision, for, when you understand them, you will better perceive things there, from your vision, having perceived the truth concerning that which is truly beautiful, just, and good. And this is a real vision, both for you and for us. So shall our city be inhabited, and not as an idle dream.

'Most cities are at present inhabited by such men as fight with one another about shadows, and raise sedition, as if it were some good. But the truth is otherwise. In whatever city those who are to govern are the most reluctant to undertake government, that city, of necessity, will be the best established, and the most free from sedition. And that city, whose Governors are of a contrary character, will be in a contrary condition. Do you think, Glauco, that our pupils will disobey us, when they hear these injunctions, and be unwilling to labour jointly in the city, each bearing a part, but spending the most of their time with one another, free from public affairs?

'For we are prescribing advice which is just to just men. And each of them will enter magistracy from this standpoint beyond all others. That they are under a necessity to govern in a manner contrary to all the present Governors of all other cities. If you discover a life for those who are to be our Governors, better than that of governing itself, then it will be possible for you to have the city well established. For there alone shall those govern who are truly inwardly rich, not in gold, but in that state in which a happy man should be rich, enjoying a fulfilled and happy life. But if men who are poor, and hungry, owning no goods of their own, come to the public, thinking they ought to pillage from the better-off, it is not possible to have the city rightly established. For in the contest between who shall govern, such a war being domestic, and within the people, it destroys both themselves, and the rest of the city.

'So, who else would you oblige to enter the guardianship of the city, but such as are the most acquainted with the principles by which the city is best established. Are you willing that we now consider by what means such men shall be spiritually educated, and how one shall bring them into the inward Light, the offspring of the Good, as some say, the journey from Hades, to ascend to the Gods? This now, as it seems, is not simply the turning round of a shell, but the conversion of the soul coming from some dark ignorance, to the true daylight, that is the ascent to Real Beingness, which I say is true philosophy. Ought we not to consider which of the disciplines possesses such a power?

'What then, Glauco, may that discipline of the soul be, which draws her from that which is generated by the world towards being its Real Self? Did we not say that it was necessary for them, while young, to be trained for war, in case we are called to defend the city from Barbarians and other jealous cities? It is proper that this military discipline be added to that which is now the object of our enquiry, and not to be regarded as useless except for military men. Well, they were, in our former discourse, instructed by us in gymnastics and musical harmony which benefits the soul. Gymnastics indeed respects what has been generated and knows what is to be destroyed, for it presides over the increase and decrease of bodily strength and vigour. This then cannot be the discipline which we investigate.

'Is it harmonious music, such as we formerly described?' 'But it was,' he interjected, 'a counterpart of gymnastics, if you remember, instructing our future Guardians in refined tendencies, imparting no knowledge, but only with respect to harmony and with regard to rhythm, and in discourses, certain other habits, which are the sisters of these. Such discourses as fables and allegories which bring us nearer to truth.' 'Well said, Glauco; you have, most accurately, reminded me. But what should our discipline actually be? For, all the arts have somehow been shown to be mechanical and illiberal.' 'Yet what other discipline remains distinct from music, gymnastic, and the arts?'

'Come,' I said, 'if we have nothing further besides these to take, let us take something which extends over them all, such as this general proposition, which all arts, minds, and sciences employ, and which everyone ought, in the first place, necessarily to learn. This trifling thing,' said I laughing, 'to know completely one, two, and three! I call this summarily, number, and computation. Or is it not so, with reference to these numbers, that every art, and likewise every science, must of necessity depend? And must not the art of war likewise participate in them?

'Palamedes then, in his tragedies, shows everywhere that Agamemnon, to say the least, was a most ridiculous general. For haven't you noticed how he says, that having invented numeration, he adjusted the ranks in the camp at Troy, and numbered both the ships, and all the other forces, as if they were not numbered before. And then Agamemnon, so it seems, did not even know how many foot soldiers he had, since he didn't understand how to count them. So what kind of General do you imagine him to be?' 'An absurd one, if this were true, and not a dramatist's invention.' 'Is there any other discipline then,' I said, 'which we shall establish to be more necessary for a military man, than to be able to compute and to number?' 'This most of all, if he would any way understand how to best martial his troops, and still more if he is to be a heroic man.' 'Do you see, with regard to this question of discipline the same as I do? That it seems to belong to those virtues which we are investigating, which naturally lead to intelligence, but that no one uses it rightly as being a fine conductor towards Real Being. I shall endeavour to explain my opinion in this manner.

'With reference to those qualities which I distinguish within myself such as lead towards intelligence, please consider them along with me, and either agree or dissent, in order that we may more distinctly see whether this be truly as I conjecture regarding this question.' 'Show me, then.' 'I shall, if you take with me, some questions which have a relation to the senses, and are determined by them.' 'You plainly mean such things as appear at a distance, and such as are painted.' 'You have not altogether, apprehended my meaning.

'These classes call upon intelligence, which issue from a contrary sensation at one and the same time. And such as issue in this way, I believe to be those which call upon intelligence, since here sense manifests the one sensation no less than its contrary, whether it meets with it nearby, or at a distance. But you will understand my meaning more plainly in this manner if I give you an example. These, we say, are three fingers, [I held them up], the little finger, the one next to it, and the middle ring finger. Consider then, speaking about them when they are seen nearby, and take notice of this fact concerning them.

'Each of them alike appears to be a finger, and in this there is no difference, whether it is seen in the middle or in the end, whether it is white or brown, thick or slender, or anything else of this kind. For in all these objects, the soul is under no necessity to question through the intellect as to what is a finger. For never does sight alone, at the same time intimate finger to be finger, and its contrary. Well, with reference to their being greater and smaller, the sight sufficiently perceives this, and it makes no difference to it, that one of them is situated in the middle, or at the end; similarly, with reference to their thickness and slenderness, their softness and hardness. Does the sense of touch sufficiently perceive these things, and in like manner the other senses; do they in any way defectively manifest such sensations? Or does each of them act efficiently in this matter?

'First of all, must not that sense which relates to hardness, necessarily relate to softness, and it reports to the soul, as if one and the same, that the same finger is both hard and soft when it feels this to be so. And must not the soul, in such cases, of necessity be in doubt, when the sense points out it is hard, since it calls the same thing soft and likewise; and so with reference to the sense relating to lightness and heaviness. The soul must be in doubt as to what is light and what is heavy, if the sense intimates that heavy is light, and that light is heavy.

'It is likely that first of all, in such cases, the soul, calling on reason and intelligence, endeavours to discover whether the things reported are one, or whether they be two. And if they appear to be two, each of them appears to be one, and distinct from the other. And if each of them be one, and both of them two, he will by intelligence perceive two distinct objects, for, if they were not distinct, he could not perceive two, but only one. The sight in like manner, we say, perceives large and small, but not as distinct from each other, but as something that is confused, does it not? In order to achieve clarity in this matter, intelligence is obliged again to consider largeness and smallness, not as confused, but as distinct, after a manner contrary to the sense of sight. And is it not from here, somehow, that it begins to question what is large, and what is small? And so we have called the one questioning faculty intelligible, and the other the visible.

'This then is what I am now endeavouring to express, when I said that some things call on the mind, and others do not. And some perceptions fall on the senses at the same time as their contraries. I define that one discriminative faculty to be such as requires intelligence, but such visual faculties do not excite intelligence. It is with reference to number and unity, Glauco, to which of the two classes do you think they belong?' 'I do not understand.'

'Try to reason by analogy, from what we have already said, for, if unity be of itself sufficiently seen, or be apprehended by any other sense, it will not lead towards Real Being, as we said concerning the finger analogy. But if there always is seen at the same time something contrary to it, so that it shall no more appear to be a unity, then it would require someone to judge it. And the soul would be under a compulsion to doubt within itself, and to enquire, arousing this conception within itself, and to investigate what this unity is. And so the discipline which relates to unity would be of the class of those categories which lead, and turn the soul towards the contemplation of Real Being.' 'But indeed this at least,' he said, 'is what the very sight of it effects in no small degree. For we behold the same thing, at one and the same time as one, when we contrast it with an infinite multitude.'

'And if this be the case with reference to unity,' I said, 'will not every number be affected in the same manner?' 'Of course, but surely both computation and arithmetic wholly relate to number.' 'Very much so.' 'These then seem to point to truth?' 'Yes, for number belongs, to those disciplines which we are investigating. For the soldier must necessarily learn these skills, for the best disposition of his ranks; and the philosopher for the attaining to the apperception of Real Being, emerging from inborn intuition, or he can never become one capable of reason. And our Guardian at least should be both a soldier and a philosopher.

'It is proper, Glauco, to establish by law this discipline, and to persuade those who are to manage the greatest affairs of the city to apply themselves to arithmetical computation, and study it, not in a childish way, but until by intelligence itself, they arrive at the contemplation of the very nature of numbers. Not for the sake of buying or selling, as merchants and retailers, but for war, and for the facility in the conversion of the soul itself, towards realization of truth and essence. And now, I perceive similarly that at present while this discipline respecting computations is mentioned, how beautiful it is, and in every way advantageous towards our purpose, if one applies it for the sake of knowledge, and not with a view to commerce!

'This very approach, which we now mention, how rigorously does it lead the soul, and compel it to reason about number in itself? By no means conceding that a man engaged in such reasoning will visualize numbers which have visible and tangible forms! For you know already that some of those who are skilled in this practice, know that if a man in reasoning should attempt to divide unity itself, they would ridicule him. But if you divide numbers into parts, they multiply them, afraid lest unity should appear not to be unity, but multiplicity. What do you think now, Glauco, if one should ask one of them, "My good sirs, on what kind of numbers are you reasoning in which there is unity, such as you think fit to approve, each whole equal being equal to each whole, and not differing in the smallest degree, having no part in itself?" What do you think they would answer?' 'I suppose, that they would mean such numbers that can only be conceived by the mind alone, but cannot be comprehended in any other way.'

'You see, my dear friend, that in reality this disciplinary exercise appears to be necessary for us, since it seems to compel the soul to employ intelligence itself in the perception of truth. And surely it effects this aim to a very powerful degree. Again, have you ever considered this? That those who are naturally skilled in computation appear to be acute in all disciplines, and such as are naturally slow, if they be instructed and exercised in this skill, although they derive no other advantage, yet at the same time all of them proceed to become more acute than they were before? And definitely, you will not easily find any study which occasions greater labour to the student than this. On all these accounts this discipline is not to be omitted, but the best minds are to be instructed in it.

'Let one thing be clearly established among us and, in the next place, let us consider if that which is consequent to our agreement, in any respect appertains to us.' 'What is it, do you mean geometry?' 'Yes, Glauco, right on the mark!' 'As far as it relates to military activities, it is plain that it belongs to us, for planning encampments, the occupation of ground, contracting and extending an army, and all those formations into which they shape troops, both in battles and on marches. It would make all the difference to the general, if he is a geometrician. But surely for such purposes as ours, a little geometry and some degree of computation might suffice, but we must enquire, whether a great deal of it, and great advances in it, would contribute anything worthwhile to our great end, to make us more easily perceive the idea of the Good.

'And we say that everything contributes to this that obliges the soul to turn, both immanently and transcendentally, towards that region in which the divinity of Beingness, dwells, which the soul must by all means know. If therefore it compels the soul to contemplate essence, it belongs to us, but if it obliges it to contemplate that which generates from the mind, it does not belong to us. Those who are even a little conversant in geometry, will not dispute with us over this point; that this science is perfectly contrary to the common modes of speech employed in it by those who practise it. They speak somehow most ridiculously, in all their discourses, which seem to be with a view to operation, and to worldly practice. Thus they speak of making a square, of prolonging, of adjoining, and the like. As if the whole of this discipline should only be studied for the sake of mundane knowledge. But truly, it is the knowledge of that which always *Is* or sheer Existence, and not that which is sometimes generated by the mind and subject to being destroyed.

'It would seem that geometry, dear Glauco, draws the soul towards truth, and to produce a mental energy adapted to a philosopher, so as to raise his power of the soul to higher realms, instead of causing it improperly, as at present, just to contemplate things below. As often as possible then, we should give orders, that those in this most beautiful city of ours by no means omit geometry, for even its subsidiary works are not inconsiderable.' 'What subsidiary works?' 'Those, which you mentioned relating to the army; and with reference to all disciplines, as to the understanding of them more adequately, such as architecture, building, map making, garden layout, city planning and so on. We know somehow, that those who have learned geometry make a great difference to life. Let us then establish this second discipline for our youth.

'Furthermore, shall we, in the third place, establish astronomy? Or are you of a different opinion?' 'I am, for to be well skilled in the seasons of months and years belongs only to agriculture and navigation, and the military art.' 'You seem to be afraid of public opinion, lest you should appear to encourage useless disciplines. But astronomy is not contemptible, although it is difficult to persuade people differently, that by each of these disciplines a certain organ of the soul is purified and resuscitated, when it is blinded and buried by studies of another kind. The soul is a faculty more worth saving than a thousand eyes, since truth is perceived by this faculty alone. To such as have never observed that, they will probably think you say nothing worthwhile at all, for they see no other advantage in these studies worthy of attention.

'Come then,' I said, 'let us go back over this again, for we have not rightly considered all that which follows on from geometry. For example, after a plain surface, we have taken a solid, moving in a circle, before we considered it by itself. But if we had proceeded correctly we should have taken the third extension, immediately after the second. For that is what one may call the increase of cubes, and what ascertains their thickness.' 'Yes, but these problems, Socrates, do not seem to have been discovered yet.'

'The reason for it,' I said, 'is twofold. Because there is no city which sufficiently honours them, they are slightly regarded, the subject being considered to be too difficult.

Besides which, those who investigate this science need a teacher, without which they cannot discover its value. And a competent teacher is hard to find, and when he is found, as things are at present, those who are appointed to investigate these sciences, as they conceive so pompously of themselves, will not obey them. But if the whole city presided over these enquiries, and held them in esteem, all those who studied them would be obedient. Then their investigations, being carried on with assiduity and vigour, would reveal themselves for what they really were. Since even now, while they are on the one hand despised and rejected by the multitude, and on the other by those who study them without being able to give any account of their utility. Yet, under all these disadvantages, the people increase through their native grace, and it is wonderful that they do so.' 'Truly,' he said, 'this grace is most remarkable. But tell me more clearly what you were just saying, for somehow that study which respects a plain surface you call geometry. And then, you mentioned astronomy in the next place, but afterwards you drew back.'

'Because, when I am hastening to discuss things rapidly, I actually advance more slowly. The increase of thickness was considered, that we passed over, because the common method of treating it is ridiculous; and after geometry we mentioned astronomy. We then established astronomy as the fourth discipline, if the city shall approve it, Glauco.' 'Now if you agree with me, Socrates, I shall proceed in my commendation of astronomy, which you formerly reproved as superficial. For it is evident, I conceive, to everyone, that this discipline compels the soul to examine and study all that is in the heavens above, and the influences they conduct here on Earth.' 'It is probable,' I said, 'that it is evident to everyone but to me. For to my mind it does not appear so. In the manner it is now pursued by those who introduce it into philosophy, it entirely causes the soul to look downwards.' 'On what do you base that statement?'

'You seem to me, Glauco, to have formed an ignoble opinion of the disciplines respecting that which is higher, and what they are. For you seem to imagine that if anyone contemplates the various bodies in the firmament, by earnestly looking up at the night sky, you think that he has intelligent knowledge concerning these phenomena, and does not merely see them with his eyes. But perhaps you judge rightly, and I am foolishly wrong. For, I am not able to conceive that any other discipline can make the soul look upwards, but that which respects Beingness, and the invisible. And if a man undertakes to learn anything about sensible objects, whether he looks upwards with mouth gaping, or downwards with mouth shut, never shall I admit that he has truly learns, according to my criteria. For I affirm that he has not found a true science of these phenomena, as I say that his soul does not look upwards, but downwards, even though he might float as he learns, lying on his back, either on land or at sea.' 'I am punished, Socrates, for you have justly rebuked me. But which is the proper way, in your opinion, of studying astronomy, which is different from the methods adopted at present, if they intend to learn it with advantage, for the purposes we speak about?'

'In this manner,' I said, 'that those varied beauties in the heavens, in so far as they are embroidered in a visible object, be regarded as most beautiful and most accurate of their kind, but far inferior to Real Beingness. For those orbits in which real velocity, and real slowness, in true number, and in all true figures, are carried out mechanically with respect to one another, and carry all forces that are within them. They, truly, are to be comprehended by reason and the mind, but not by intelligence, or do you think they can? Is it not the case that artistic beauty in the heavens should be made use of as a paradigm for learning about Real things, in the same manner as one should look at beautiful symmetrical geometrical figures, drawn remarkably well and elaborately by Dædalus, or some other fine artist or painter? For a man who was skilled in geometry, on seeing these, would truly think the workmanship was most excellent, yet would esteem it ridiculous to consider these things seriously as Real in the philosophic sense of the word, as if from them he would be able to learn the truth as to what they were in single, in duplicate, or in any other proportion.

'And don't you also think that he who is truly an astronomer will be affected in the same manner, when he looks up at the orbits of the planets? And that he will reckon that the heavens, and all bodies in them, are created by the artificer of the heavens, in the most beautiful manner possible, for such works to be established. But would not he consider it to be absurd, whoever should imagine that this proportion of night with day, and of both these to a month, and of a month to a year, and of other stars to similar chronology, towards one another, existed always in the same manner, and in no way suffered any change; although they have a body, and are visible, and they search by every method to apprehend the truth of these things?

'Let us then make use of problems,' said I, 'in the study of astronomy, as in geometry. And let us dismiss the heavenly bodies, if we intend truly to apprehend astronomy, and render profitable, instead of unprofitable, that part of the soul which is naturally wise.' 'You truly encourage a much harder task on astronomers, than is placed on them at present.' 'And I think,' I replied, 'that we must likewise regard other sciences, in the same way, if we are to be of any service as law-givers. But can you suggest any more of the proper disciplines?' 'I cannot suggest any more,' he replied, 'at present.'

'It appears to me, that not only one, but many forms of discipline, are afforded by this science of motion. All of which any wise man can probably know. Those which occur to me are two. Together with the one named already, there is its counterpart. As the eyes seem to be suited to astronomy, so the ears seem to be suited to harmonious music, as is the soul. And these seem to be sister sciences, one with another, both as the Pythagoreans say, and we, Glauco, agree with them. So how shall we progress? Shall we not, since this is their great work, enquire how they speak about them, and, if there be any other matters besides these, enquire into them likewise? But above all, we should still guard that which is our own method. That those we educate never attempt at any time to learn any of those sciences in an imperfect manner, and are always aiming at that excellence to which all should be directed, as we have now referred to, in discussing astronomy.

'For, do you know that they make the same enquiries with regard to harmony, as with astronomy? For, while they measure one with another, the symphonies and sounds which are heard, they work at, like the astronomers, somewhat unprofitably.' 'By heavens, yes,' he said, 'and ridiculously too, while they frequently repeat certain notes, and listen with their ears to catch the sound as from a neighbouring place. And some of them say they hear some middle note, but that the interval which measures them is the smallest, and others again doubt this, and say that the notes are the same as were sounded before. So both parties subject the intellect to the delight of their ears.' 'But you speak, Glauco,' I said, 'of those mercenary musicians, who perpetually harass and torment their strings, and rack them on the pegs. But that the comparison may not be too tedious, I shall say nothing of the blows given by the prong, or the accusations made against the strings, their refusals and stubbornness, but bring that image to an end, and say we ought not to choose these persons to speak about harmony; but only those true musicians whom we mentioned. For these minds do the same things here as the others do in astronomy; for in these symphonies which they compose, they search for numbers, but they do not pass on to the problems, to enquire which numbers are harmonious, and which are not, and the reason why they are neither the one nor the other.'

'You speak,' he said, of a superhuman work.' 'Not exactly, but profitable, for the search of the Beautiful and Good. But if pursued in a mercenary manner it is unprofitable. But I think that the proper method of enquiry into all these things is to reach the happy communion and alliance with each other, and then reason in what respects they are concordant with one another. That will contribute some knowledge to what we require, and our quest will not be in vain, otherwise it will. I, myself, teach in this same way.' 'But you speak, Socrates, of a very mighty work.' 'Do you mean the introduction to it, or what else? Or do you not know that all these matters are introductory to the law itself which we ought to learn. For even those that are expert in this teaching, do not appear to be skilled in dialectic.' 'No, indeed, except a very few, of all that I have met with.' 'But while they are unable, to employ and receive reason, will they ever be able to know anything of what we say is necessary to be understood, or not?' 'Never will they be able to do this work.'

'Is not this itself, Glauco, the law? To give perfection to dialectic, which being intelligible, may be said to be imitated by the power of sight, which endeavours, as we observed, first to look at animals, then at the stars, and last of all at the Sun itself. So when anyone attempts to discuss a subject without any of the senses operating, by pure reasoning, he is impelled to that which is particular, and if he does not give up until he apprehends it by his own supreme intelligence which is the Good itself. He then arrives at the end of the intelligible, as the other does at the end of the visible. Now, do you call this progression the dialectic?' 'What else?'

'And now, as in our former comparative allegory, you had the liberation from chains, and turning from the shadows towards images and the light, and an ascent from the cavern to the Sun. And then there is the inability at first to behold animals and plants, and the light of the Sun, but only reflections in water are seen. These reflections are merely the shadows of Real things in themselves, the shadows of images, shadowed by another light, which is itself a shadow as compared with the Sun. In the same way, the arts and sciences, which we have discussed, have this power, to lead up to all this understanding of that which is best in and for the soul, and to the contemplation of that which is best, in Beingness.' 'I accept all that, but it seems to me to be extremely difficult to engage with them, and in another respect it is difficult not to engage with them.' 'But, we shall hear about these teachings not only now as at present, but often again, to discuss them, in order to establish these matters as they are now expressed.

'Let us go to the law itself, and discuss it in the same way as we have finished this introduction. Think, then, what is the mode of the power of the dialectic, and into what qualities is it divided, and what are the paths leading up to it? For these considerations, it is most likely, will conduct us to that place at which, when we arrive, we shall find a resting place, and the end of our journey. You will, eventually, friend Glauco, be able to see the image of that of which we are reasoning about, the truth itself. This is what, to me at least, it seems to be, whether it is in reality or not. It is not proper, strenuously to affirm, but it is something of this kind that must be strenuously affirmed. And furthermore, that it is the power of dialectic alone, which can discover this, by one who is skilled in that which we have discussed, and that, by no other method is it possible. This also, we may strenuously affirm. This, at least, no one will dispute with us, for no other method can attempt to comprehend, in any orderly way, what each particular Being is in itself; for all the other arts, sciences and philosophies respect either the opinions or desires of men.

'Those others, which we said participate in some aspect of Being, like geometry, and such, are connected with truth. But it is impossible for them to have a true vision, so long as they leave the hypotheses they use unexamined; without being able to assign any reason for their existence. For where the basic principle is unknown, and the conclusion and intermediate steps are connected with an unknown principle, by what contrivance can it become a real science? Does not the dialectic method, and no other, proceed in a correct way, to the principle itself, removing all hypotheses, that it may firmly establish truth, and gradually drawing and leading the eye of the soul upwards, when it was formerly buried in a barbaric mire. We should use the arts as assistants and handmaids in this attempt, which through custom we frequently call sciences, but which really need another name more like opinion, as they are more obscure than true science?

'We have somewhere in the former part of our discourse termed it the Mind. But this controversy is not, it seems to me, about a name, with those who enquire into matters of such great importance, as those now before us. Do you agree then, as formerly, to call the first part, science, the second, understanding, the third, faith, and the fourth, conjecture? And both of these last two are opinion? And the first two are intelligence? And that opinion is employed concerning generation from the mind, and intelligence from essence? Similarly as essence is to generation, so is intelligence to opinion, science to faith, and the understanding to conjecture? But as for the analogy of that major power which these minor powers respect, and the twofold division of each, that is the object of opinion, and of the intellect. These we omit, dear Glauco, that we may not spend longer time and be more wordy here than in our former reasoning.

'But don't you call him skilled in dialectic, who apprehends the reason of the essence of each particular? And as for the man who is not able to give a reason to himself, and to another, would you not say that he lacks intelligence of the essence of each particular? And is not the case the same with reference to the Good? Whosoever cannot define it by reason, separating the idea of the Good from all other extraneous ideas, as in a battle, piercing thoroughly through all arguments, eagerly striving to confute, not according to opinion, but according to essence; and in all these steps, resolutely marching forward with the undeviating power of pure reason. Such a one, who treads another path, knows nothing of the Good itself, nor of any real goodness whatsoever. And if he has formed any conception of the Good, we must say he has attained it by opinion, not by science. And that in the present life he is sleeping, and living in dreams, and that before he is aroused he will descend to Hades, and there be profoundly and perfectly laid asleep.

'So surely, you will not, I trust, allow your own children whom you nourish and educate in reasoning, without understanding the idea of the essential Good, and let them have the supreme government of the most important affairs in the State, while they remain irrational as dumb posts. You will then lay down this to them as a law. That in a most special way they attain to that part of education, by which they may be able to question and answer in the most scientific manner. Does it seem to you, that the banner of dialectic is to be hoisted on high, as a defence against all other inferior disciplines? And that no other discipline can with propriety be raised higher than this; and that everything respecting sound discipline is now attained?

'Now, to whom shall we assign these disciplines, and in what way? Do you remember then our former election of rulers, what manner of man we chose? Recall then, that those were not the only reasons why these particular best natures should be chosen. Not only are the most firm and brave to be preferred, and, as far as possible, the most graceful in manners. Besides, we must not only find those whose manners are generous and serious, but they must be possessed of every other natural disposition conducive to this highest education. They must have, awareness with respect to the disciplines, that they may learn them without difficulty. For, souls are much more influenced by robust disciplines, than in strenuous exercises of the body. For it is the soul's proper work, and one which is not held in common with the body, but more confined to the soul.

'And we must look for candidates with a good memory, sturdy, and in every way energetic. Or how else do you think anyone will be willing to endure the fatigue of the body, and to accomplish at the same time such learning and study? The mistakes about philosophy, and the contempt for it, have arisen for the neglect of these reasons; because, as I formerly said, if philosophy is not applied in a manner worthy of its dignity, it ought never to have been applied at all, especially by those whom I would term bastardly. But only the legitimate heirs should pursue the Queen of the Sciences. In the first place, he who is to apply himself to real philosophy, and not pseudo philosophy or sophistry, ought not to be deficient in his love of effort and attention, and should not be half-hearted and lazy, which takes place when a man mainly loves wrestling and hunting, and all different kinds of sports and exercises of the body too much, and is not a true lover of learning. Such a man, neither wishes to hear nor enquire, and in all these respects has a built-in aversion to labour.

'And shall we not regard that soul as maimed to truth, which easily admits the involuntary lie. And, although at any time he is found to be ignorant, he is not displeased with himself, but like a wild boar willingly wallows in ignorance? And also, as with temperance, fortitude, magnanimity, and all the categories of virtue, we must carefully ignore the bastardly, and attend to the legitimate. For when any private person or city fails to understand how to judge all these things, unawares, they employ the lame and the bastardly, for whatever they have need to achieve. Private persons employ them as tutors, and some cities as Governors. We must beware of all such dangers. For, if we only take those who are whole and sound in body and mind for such extensive learning and exercises, and then instruct them, then Justice herself will not blame us, and we shall preserve both the city and its constitution. But if we introduce persons of a different persuasion into these matters, we shall do everything the incorrect way, and bring philosophy under still greater ridicule than it already is.

'But I myself seem at present to sound somewhat ridiculous. I forgot that we were amusing ourselves, and spoke with too great an emphasis. For, while I was speaking, I looked towards philosophy; and seeing her most unworthily abused, I seem to have been filled with indignation, and, becoming enraged at those who are the cause of it, I spoke too earnestly in what I said. But let us not forget this; that in our election of Guardians, we decided to make the choice of elder men, but in now it will not be allowed. For we must believe Solon, who taught that one who is growing old is able to learn many things, but he is less able to put this knowledge into effect, than to run. All mighty and numerous labours belong to the young! Everything then relating to arithmetic and geometry, and all that previous instruction which they should be taught before they learn dialectic, ought to be set before them while they are youths, and that method of teaching observed, which will make them learn without compulsion.

'A free man ought never to learn discipline under the condition of slavery; for the labours of the body when endured through compulsion make the body feel worse; but voluntary discipline, endures in the soul. Do not compel boys in their learning, but train them, amusing themselves, that you may be better able to observe to where the genius of each naturally tends. Don't you remember, that we said the boys are even to be carried to war, as spectators, on horseback, and that they are to be brought near, if they can with safety, to the centre of the battle, and like young hunting hounds taste blood? Whoever shall appear the most advanced in all these labours, disciplines, and trials, are to be selected into a certain group.' 'At what age?' 'When they have finished their necessary exercises, for during this time, while that continues, for two or three years, it is impossible to accomplish anything else, as fatigue and sleep are the great enemies of learning. And this too is not the least of their trials, but we must see what character each of them has, in performing his exercises.

'And after this period, let those who have been selected, around the age of twenty, receive greater honours than the others. And let those disciplines, which in their youth they learned separately, be brought before them into one perspective, that they may see the agreement of all the disciplines, one with the other, and with the nature of Real Being. And this is the greatest trial for distinguishing between those minds who are naturally fitted for dialectic, and those who are not. He who perceives this concordance of disciplines will be skilled in dialectic; he who does not, will be not! It will then be necessary for you, after you have observed all these tendencies well, and seen who are the most qualified among them, being stable in their disciplines, and stable in war, and in the other requirements established by law, to make the choice from such, after they reach thirty years.

'You will select from those formerly chosen, and advance them to greater honours. You must likewise observe them, testing them by the trial of dialectic, so as to ascertain which of them, without the assistance of his eyes, or any other sense, is able to proceed with an intelligible enquiry into the truth of Beingness itself. And here, my friend, is a work to proceed with great caution. Don't you see the evil, which at present attends dialectic, and how great it is? The lawlessness, which seems to infect it. Are you not surprised at this state of things and will you not forgive them? Just as if a certain adopted child, was educated in great opulence by a rich and noble family, believing he was their offspring, and flattered, and should learn when reaching manhood that he was not descended from those who are said to be his parents. And then should discover his real parents; can you not see how such a man would be affected both towards his flatterers, and towards his supposed parents, both at the time when he knew nothing of the deception, and at that time when he came to discover it?

'I prophesy then, that he will pay more honour to his father and mother, and his other supposed relations, than to the flatterers, and he will not neglect them when they are in any want. And be less apt to do or say anything amiss to them; and in matters of consequence be less disobedient to them than to those flatterers, than during that period in which he was ignorant of the truth. But when he perceives the real state of affairs, I again prophesy, he will then slacken in his honour and respect for the real parents and the foster parents, and attend to the flatterers, and be more persuaded by them now than he was formerly. And live according to their manner, conversing with them openly. But for the real father, and those supposed parents, if he is not of an entirely good natural disposition, he will have no longer any regard.'

'But in what way does this comparison respect those who are conversant with dialectic?'

'We have certain dogmas inherited from our childhood concerning things we believe to be just and beautiful, on which we have been nourished by our parents, obeying and honouring them. Are there not other pursuits similar to these, with pleasures, flattering our souls, and drawing them towards them? They do not however persuade those who are in any degree temperate; who honour their relations, and obey them. What now, when to one who has been so affected, this question is proposed, "What is the Beautiful?" and when he answers what he has heard from the lawgiver, he is refuted by false reasoning. For false reasoning frequently, and in every way, convincing him, reduces him to the opinion that this or that is no more beautiful than if it is deformed; and in the same way, as to what is just and good, and whatever else he held in high esteem. What do you think such a one will do, after this, with regard to these relationships, as for honouring and obeying them?' 'Of necessity,' he said, 'he will neither honour nor obey them any longer in the same way as before.'

'Yes, when he no longer thinks that this attitude is honourable, and related to him as it was formerly, and cannot discover those values which really exist, is it possible he can readily join himself to any other life than the flattering one?' 'It is not possible, and from being an observer of the law, he shall, I think, seem to be a transgressor.' 'Yes, is it not likely that those who are affected in this way, and who in this situation apply themselves to reasoning, should work to earn forgiveness?' 'And pity.' 'You take care, unless this compassionate case befalls many of the age of thirty. They ought then by every method to apply themselves to reasoning?

'And is not this comparison one that cautions prudence? That they do not taste pure reasoning, while they are young, for have you not forgotten, that youth, when they first taste logical reasoning, abuse it in the way of amusement, and they use it always for the purpose of contradiction. And imitating those who are refuters, they themselves refute others, delighting like whelps in dragging and tearing their quarry to pieces, those who are near and dear to them. And after they have confronted many in debate, and have themselves been confronted by many objections, do they not vehemently and speedily set aside all the opinions they formerly possessed? And by this waywardness, they themselves, and the whole of philosophy, is slandered by others.

'But he who is of a riper, more mature age, will not be disposed to take part in such madness, but will rather imitate the philosopher who inclines to reason and enquire after truth, than one who, for the sake of diversion, amuses himself, and indulges in contradiction. He will no doubt become more modest himself, and render the practice of disputation more honourable instead of being dishonourable. Are not all our former remarks rightly made, in the way of a warning, as to this adolescent tendency, that those philosophic natures should be both decent and stable, to whom the science of the dialectic is to be imparted? But not as at present, when every vulgar nature, and such as are not at all fit, are admitted to participate. Is it then sufficient for a man to remain in acquiring the art of dialectic with perseverance and application, and doing nothing else, just as he did when he was exercising himself in all bodily exercises, and for double the time which he spent on these?

'After this you must compel them to descend to that prison house of a cave again, and oblige them to educate themselves relating to war, and such other magistracies, as they require youth to do, that they may not fall short of others, even in worldly experience. And they must be still further tested among these subjects, when being drawn to every different quarter by attractions, to see if they will continue firmly, or whether they will in any way be drawn aside.' 'And for how long a time, do you require this service?' 'For about fifteen years. And when they reach the age of fifty, such of them as are in good health, and have excelled in all these activities, in deeds, and in the sciences, are now to be led to the end. Now they are obliged to incline the ray of their soul's gaze towards that which imparts Light to everything; and, when they have known the Good in itself, to use it as a paradigm, each of them, in their turn, adorning both the city and private citizens, and themselves, will serve during the remainder of their lives.

'For the most part, they must be occupied in philosophy; and when it is their turn, they must toil in political affairs, and take on the responsibility of government, each for the good of the city, performing this office, not as something prestigious, but as something that is very necessary. And after they have educated others in the same manner, and left men and women behind them like themselves to be the future Guardians of the city, they will depart to inhabit the islands of the blest. But the city will publicly erect monuments in their honour, and offer sacrifices, if the oracle assents, as are granted to superior beings, who are both happy and divine men.' 'You have Socrates, like a sculpture, turned our Governors into most admirable figures.' 'And our Governesses too, Glauco, for do not suppose that I have spoken, any more about the men than the women, such among them as are of sufficient genius, of course.' 'Right,' said Glauco, 'they are to share in all things equally with men, as we are all related, as children of the Gods.'

'Do you agree that with reference to the city and republic,

we have really only spoken about what can only be regarded as pious hopes, but such projects are indeed difficult, yet possible, to achieve. And in no other way than this has it been adequately described. That is, when those who are truly philosophers, whether several of them or a single one, become Governors in such a city, they shall despise the present system of honours, considering them illiberal and of no value; but esteeming rectitude and the honours which are derived from that virtue, above all. They must see the just, in all other men and women, the greatest and most necessary virtue. And they should minister to them, and encourage them to thoroughly regulate the constitution of their own city.

'As many of those in the city who are above the age of ten, they should send into the country, removing their children away from those vulgar habits which their parents possess at present. There they will be educated in our own way according to our laws, which we have formerly outlined. So, the city and republic we have described will be established in the speediest and easiest manner. The city will both be happy in itself, and be of the greatest advantage to those people among whom it is established.' 'Very much so. And you seem to me, Socrates, to have described very well how this city shall arise, if and when it arises at all.' 'Are not now these discourses sufficient concerning such a city as this republic, and concerning the men and women to be educated in its likeness? For it is now evident what kind of men and women they ought to be, eh Glauco?' 'It is evident, Socrates, that your enquiry seems to me to be almost completed.

BOOK 8

POLITICAL SYSTEMS
COMPARED

'So be it, dear, Glauco, we have now agreed that in our ideal city, which is to be established in the most perfect way possible, the women, children and the whole of their education and employment in peace and war is to be held in common, as we have already discussed. And their Kings or Philosopher Guardians are to be such as they excel all others both in philosophy, wisdom and the arts of military science.' Glauco interrupted, 'Socrates, I truly wish to know what it is you mean by the four polities.' 'You shall hear that from me without any difficulty. For they are these which I will mention, and they have names too.

'There is that polity which is commended by many, called the Cretan and the Spartan. There is, secondly, that which has some praise, called Oligarchy, but a polity full of many evils, which is different from this that follows next in order, called Democracy. Then there is Tyranny, which is very different from all these. That is the fourth and final disease to befall a city. We have already discussed that which resembles Aristocracy, which we have rightly pronounced to be both approaching the good and the just. So we are now to go over the worst systems. There is the contentious and the ambitious man, who is formed according to the Spartan polity, resembling an Oligarchy; and then the Democratic model and the Tyrannical. The Tyrannical is the most unjust, and is opposed to the most just.

'But let us first consider in what way a Timocracy would arise out of an Aristocracy. Although the Governors shall install the best men among them in office, they nevertheless sometimes being found unworthy of it, and coming to have the power their fathers possessed, will soon begin to be negligent in their Guardianship; because they do not esteem the great power of harmonious music to influence their souls, as they should, and in the same way the important gymnastic exercises for the health of the body. So our youth will become less acquainted with the beauties of harmonious music, which benefits the mild temperament. Also the Guardians which shall be appointed from among them will not be complete Guardians. And when these men govern, wherever they prevail, they perpetually generate war and enmity. To such a race of men as this, we predict that they will say that there is sedition whenever protest happens to rise, which is certain to happen.'

'Shall not this polity fall somewhere in the middle, between an Aristocracy and an Oligarchy?' 'Certainly. Well, in this way, change are afraid to rebellion will happen. But in this polity, they are afraid to bring wise men into the magistracy, as no longer being able to find any such men that are truly straightforward, but of a mixed kind, in that they incline towards those who are more boisterous and simple-minded, and whose natural genius is much more fitted for war than peace. And so they esteem war's tricks and stratagems, and spend the whole of their time in continual warfare. In all other respects it does not have many features peculiar to itself, as it is unaccompanied by reason and philosophy, and honouring, if anything, gymnastics much more than harmonious music. And such masters will be harsh towards their slaves, despising them, as all do, who are badly educated.

'They will be mild towards freemen, and extremely submissive to the Governors. They are lovers of dominion and power, not thinking it proper to govern by eloquence, nor any virtue of that kind, but by warlike deeds and shows of force, being themselves lovers of wrestling and hunting. This indeed is the temper of that polity. And the older they grow, the more their people will always value money, because they are of the covetous kind, and are not sincerely aware of what constitutes true virtue, because they are destitute of the best Guardian.' 'Of what Guardian?' said Adimantus. 'Reason, accompanied by harmonious music, which being the chief inbred preservative of virtue, stays with the possessor throughout the whole of his or her life.

'It would be an Oligarchy, I think, which succeeds this polity. That polity, which is based on men's valuation of wealth, in which the rich bear rule, and the poor have no share in the government themselves. As contentious and ambitious men, they will all become lovers of gain and acquisition. They will praise and admire the rich, and bring them into the magistracy; but the poor man they will despise. They will regulate their Oligarchic power according to their quantity of wealth, more to the more wealthy, and less to the less; intimating that he who has not a certain amount of wealth settled by law, is to have no share in the government. And at the same time they are unwilling to advance money for public service, through a natural inclination towards covetousness. Have you never seen poor people in cities under Oligarchic government?' 'They are almost all poor,' he said, 'except the Governors.' 'Isn't then the city which is ruled under an Oligarchy like this, and hasn't it such evils as these, and probably more too?

'Democracy is the next to be considered. Firstly, in what manner it arises, and what kind of character it has when it has arisen. Here battle takes place between a rich man bred in the shadows, and swollen with a great deal of casually acquired flesh, through over-indulgence in food and drink, and we see him panting for breath and in agony! A Democracy arises when the poor rise up against the rich, kill some of them, banish others, and take their places in the republic, and divide the magistracies up among the remainder, which are disposed of by lot. This, truly, is the establishment of a Democracy, whether it arises by force of arms, or from others withdrawing through fear. In what way now do these live, and what sort of a State is this? For it is clear that a man of this kind will seem to be a truly Democratic man. But Democracy breeds demagogues.

'It is clear, is it not, that this city, in the first place, is full of freedom of action, speech, and of liberty, to live as anyone inclines? So far, so good. And wherever there is liberty, it is clear that everyone will regulate his own method of life in whatever way he pleases. And I think that in such a polity, most especially, there will arise men of all different kinds. How can it be otherwise? This seems, at first glance, to be one of the finest of all polities. As a variegated robe diversified with all kinds of colours, so this polity, variegated with all sorts of manners, appears the finest. And it is likely that the multitude judges this polity to be the best, like children and women, they enjoy gazing at variegated things. And it is very proper to search for a polity in such a state as this, because it contains all kinds of polities on account of its liberty; and it appears necessary for anyone who wants to constitute a good city, as we do at present, to come to a Democratic city, as to a country fair of polities, and choose that form which he most favours. Well then, isn't this a sweet manner of life for the present times. Democracy appears, a pleasant sort of polity, that is anarchical, and variegated, distributing a certain equality to all alike without distinction, whether equal or not.

'But it remains that we discuss Tyranny, and the Tyrant. In what manner does Tyranny arise? For it is clear that the change comes from Democracy. Does not Tyranny arise in the same manner from Democracy, as Democracy does from Oligarchy? What did Oligarchy propose as its good, and according to which it is constituted? It was with a view to becoming rich, was it not? An insatiable desire of riches, and a neglect of other matters, through attention to the acquisition of wealth, inevitably destroys it, although it will struggle to preserve itself by terror and waging war against peaceful neighbours. And with reference to the extent that Democracy contains liberal elements; an insatiable thirst for them destroys it likewise?' 'But what is it you say that are the good elements?'

'Liberty! For this ideal, we are told that the most beautiful city possible is a Democracy, and that for the sake of liberty anyone who is naturally free chooses to live in it. This word, liberty, is often mentioned. Does not the insatiable desire for this so-called freedom, and the neglect of other matters, change even this republic, and prepare it to stand in need of a Tyrant? When a city is governed under a Democracy, and is thirsting after liberty, it usually happens to have bad ministers appointed, and it becomes intoxicated with an unmixed draught of liberalism beyond that which is necessary. It punishes even the Governors if they are not entirely tame, and does not afford them abundant liberty, accusing them of being corrupted, and Oligarchic. And such as are obedient to the magistrates they abuse, as willing slaves, and good for nothing. Both in private and in public, they commend and honour magistrates who resemble their subjects, and subjects who resemble their magistrates.

'Must it not necessarily follow that in such a city they arrive at the summit of liberty? And must not this inbred anarchy, my friend, descend into private families, and in the end reach even the brutes. And do you know that at length they do not respect even the laws, written or unwritten, so that no one, by any means whatsoever, may become their masters? So, this now, my friend, is that Democratic government so beautiful and proud, from which Tyranny eventually springs.' 'But what follows on from this?' 'The same canker, which, springing up as a disease, as in an Oligarchy, destroyed that system. And the same condition arises here in a greater and more powerful manner. Its licentiousness enslaves the Democracy, as in reality the doing of anything to excess often occasions a mighty swing to its opposite. Excessive liberty seems to change into nothing else but excessive slavery, both with private persons and a city. And this is plain, that whenever a Tyrant arises it is from this presiding root, and from nothing else, that he blossoms.

'Shall we consider now, the happiness of the man, and of the city in which such a Tyrant arises? Does he not, in the first days, and for the first season, smile benevolently, and salute everyone he meets as a brother. He says he is not a Tyrant, and promises many reforms, both in private and in public, and frees everyone from debts, and distributes land both to the people in general, and to those lackeys about him, and affects to be mild and paternal towards all? But when, I think, he has reconciled himself to some of his foreign enemies, and ruthlessly destroyed the others, and there is tranquillity for a time, he always raises some new wars, in order that the people may be in need of a leader like himself.

'And is it not like this, that being rendered poor by payment of taxes, they become under a necessity of becoming dependent for their daily sustenance on him, and are less ready to conspire against him? And, I think, if he suspects that any of those who are of a free spirit will not allow him to govern, then in order to have some pretext for destroying them, he exposes them as an enemy and imprisons or executes them summarily. And, while he is waging fresh wars, and committing these crimes, he soon becomes hateful to his citizens. And then some of those who have been promoted along with him, and who are in power, conspire secretly against him, and among themselves, find fault with his transactions. It forces the Tyrant to eliminate all of these conspirators when he hears about them through his spies, if he means to continue to govern, until he leaves no one, either friend or foe, worth anything but as lackeys.

'Through such necessity he is truly bound, and it obliges him either to live with many depraved people, and be hated by them too, or not to live at all. And the more he is hated by his citizens whilst he commits these enormities, the more he is in need of a greater number of guards. He chooses brutal guards that he can trust, and from where shall he find them? Many depraved types of their own accord will come flying to him, if he gives them hire. What a blessed possession, if he employs such depraved but faithful men, after having destroyed his former friends! But at least he does give employment. And such companions admire him, and new citizens accompany him, but the decent men both hate and fly from him; those who are good and worthy men, who formerly placed him over them. Shall we not say modestly, that we have sufficiently shown how Tyranny arises out of Democracy, for the time being, and what it is when it does arise?' 'Yes, dear Socrates, you have shown that admirably,' he replied.

BOOK 9

EVILS OF TYRANNY

'The Tyrannical man himself, remains yet to be considered, and in what way he arises out of the Democratic system, and when he does arise, what kind of a man he is, and what kind of life does he lead, whether miserable or blessed. But, do you know what I want to discuss first? We do not seem to have sufficiently distinguished with regard to desires; of what kind they are, and how man is enslaved by them.

'Consider well what it is that I wish to know about them, for it is this. Of those pleasures and desires which are not necessary, some appear to me to be repugnant to law and these indeed seem to be inborn in everyone. But being punished by the laws, then the better desires, in conjunction with reason, either forsake some men altogether, or are less numerous and feeble. In others they grow to become more powerful, and more numerous. Such men and women are excited in sleep, when the other part of the soul, which is rational and mild, and which governs it, is fast asleep; and the part which is savage and rustic, being filled with meats and intoxicating drinks, frisks about, and driving away sleep, seeks to go and satisfy his gross desires.

'In such a one, you know, he dares to do anything, being set loose, and disengaged from all modesty and prudence. He even commits incest with anyone, whether they are mothers, sisters, Goddesses, other men, or beasts. They will even foully kill anyone, or overindulge in every kind of unclean habit. In one word, he or she is not lacking in any kind of folly or impudence. But I believe that when a man is in good health, and lives temperately, and goes to gentle sleep, having aroused his rational part, and nourished it with worthy reasoning and self-enquiry, then coming to a sense of unity within himself, allowing that part of the soul, which is longing earnestly for pleasure, neither to be starved nor glutted, so that he may lie down and rest quietly; and having likewise soothed his irascible part, not permitting it to be swept to transports of anger, or stay awake with agitated passion. Thus, having quieted these two parts of the soul, and excited the third part, in which wisdom resides, he shall in that calm manner, take rest.

'In such a man or woman one knows the truth will eventually be apprehended, and his dreams are not all repugnant to law. We have, indeed, been carried a little too far in mentioning these things, but what we want to be known is this, that there is in everyone, certain kinds of desire which are terrible, savage, and irregular, even in someone who entirely seems to us to be moderate. And these desires become most manifest in sleep.

'Well now, let's look at the formation of the Tyrannical man. Every day and night, for him there blossom forth many dreadful desires, in need of varied gratifications. Many, indeed, they commit at home, and in the city, causing a great many small mischiefs, such as stealing, burglary, pick-pocketing, stripping people of their clothes, rifling temples, making people slaves, and so on. And what is more, when they speak they sometimes turn into false informers, and give false testimony, and take bribes.' 'You could call these small mischiefs, if there are only a few such persons, Socrates.'

'What is small? What is small compared with the great? And all those tendencies, with regard to the Tyrant, when compared with the wickedness and misery of the city, do not, as the saying goes, come near the mark. For when there are many like that in the city, and others who accompany them, and when they see their own number, then these men, aided by the foolishness of the rest of the people, establish as head Tyrant the man who among them has most of their Tyrannical tendencies, and of the greatest strength within his soul. And would this Tyrannical man differ in any way similarly, when compared with the city under Tyranny, and the Democratic man, when compared with the city under Democracy? As city then is to city, as virtue is to virtue, will not man be to man, and woman be to woman, in the same way? And it is evident to everyone that there is no city more wretched than that which is under Tyranny, nor any happier than that which is under the Regal power of the Philosopher King or Guardian!

'So, come now, my good Adimantus, as a judge who pronounces after considering all matters, please kindly tell me, who, according to your opinion, is the first as to achieve happiness, and who is second, and the rest in order, there being five in all; the Regal, the Timocratic, the Oligarchic, the Democratic, and the Tyrannic?' 'The judgement, is easy, Socrates, for as if I have entered among them, I judge all of them like public performers, by their virtues and vices, and by their happiness, and its opposite.' 'Shall we then hire a herald? Or shall I myself proclaim that Adimantus, son of Ariston, has judged the best and most just man to be the happiest; and that this is the man who has most of the Regal spirit, and rules himself with a kingly power; and that the worst and the most unjust is the most wretched; and that he again happens to be the man who is most Tyrannical, who in the greatest degree tyrannizes over himself, and the city?'

'You have returned to your desire to be ironical Socrates, so let that be your proclamation!' 'Shall I add, then, whether they be known to be such or not, both to all men and to all Gods?' 'Add it, Socrates, and be done!' 'So be it, this would seem to be one proof of ours, and this, if you are of the same opinion, must be the second. Since the soul of every individual is divided into three parts, in the same manner as the city is to be divided, it will, in my opinion, admit a second proof. Of the three parts of the soul, there appear to me to be three pleasures, one peculiar to each; and three desires and governments in the same manner. There is one part, by which a man learns, and a second by which he shows an irascible spirit.

'The third is so multiform, we are unable to express it by one word peculiar to itself, but we shall name it from that which is greatest and most impetuous in it. We shall call it the Desiderative, on account of its impetuosity of desires, relative to strong meat, intoxicating wines, and venereal pleasures, and all other manner of things that belong to these laxities. And we shall call it avaricious also, because it is by no lack of wealth that such desires may be accomplished. So, if we said it rightly, we then say that its pleasure and delight are in abundance, and so shall we not reduce it under one head in our discourse. But, so as to express something meaningful to ourselves, when we make mention of this part of the soul, by calling it the covetous, and the desirous of gain, shall we not term it correctly?

'Do we not say that the spirited ought to be the ones wholly impelled to superiority, victory, and applause? If we term it the contentious and ambitious, will it not be accurately expressed? But it is evident to everyone, that the part of the soul by which we learn, is wholly intent always to know the truth. And as for wealth and glory, it cares for these least of all. When we name it desirous of learning, we shall then call it according to its proper name, the Philosophic. And do not these tendencies govern in souls, one of them in some, and others in another, as it happens? On this account then, we said there were three original types of men, the philosophic, the ambitious, and the avaricious; and that there were also three kinds of pleasures, one subject to each of these. You know then, that if you were to ask these three men, each of them separately, which of their lives is the most pleasant, each would most of all commend his own.

'And the avaricious will say that in comparison with the pleasure of acquiring wealth, that arising from honour, or from learning, is of no value, unless one makes money from it. And what says the ambitious? Doesn't he think that the pleasure arising from making money is a sort of burden? And similarly that arising from learning, unless learning brings him honour and offices of power; does he not believe it to be just smoke and mirrors? And we shall suppose the philosopher to think the other pleasures are as nothing, compared to that of knowing the truth. How is it, that while he is always employed in learning knowledge of this kind, he is not very far from pleasure? But he calls his other pleasure, needing nothing from the others, but when there is a necessity for it. When therefore, these several lives, and the respective pleasures of each, are in dispute, not with reference to living more worthily or more basely, or worse or better, but merely with reference to this need to live more pleasantly, or on the contrary more painfully, then how can we know which of them speaks more conformably to truth?

'By what means should we judge whatever is to be rightly judged? Is it not by experience, by prudence, and by reason? Or has anyone a better criterion than these? Consider now; of the three men, who is the most experienced in all the pleasures? Whether it seems to you that the avaricious man, in learning truth itself, and what it is, happens to be more experienced in the pleasures arising from knowledge than the philosopher is in that pleasure arising from the acquisition of wealth?' 'There is,' said Adimantus, 'a great difference. For the philosopher, beginning from his childhood, must, of necessity, taste the other pleasures, and what it is to know human beings, and how sweet these pleasures are. The mercenary man has no necessity of tasting, or of becoming experienced in that way, but rather, when he earnestly endeavours to achieve this, it is not an easy matter for him.'

'The philosopher then,' I replied, 'far surpasses the mercenary man, at least in his experience of all the pleasures. But what with reference to the ambitious man? Is he more experienced in the pleasures arising from honour, than the philosopher is in that arising from intellectual energy? Surely honour attends all of them, if they obtain what they aim at. For the rich man is honoured by many, so is the brave, and the wise. And, as to honour, whatever kind of pleasure it is, all of them have their own experience. But in the contemplation of Pure Being itself, what pleasure there is, it is impossible for any other than the philosopher to have tasted. On account of his experience then, he of all men judges the best. And surely, along with prudence, he alone becomes experienced. But even the faculty by which these pleasures must be judged is not the faculty of the mercenary, nor of the ambitious, but of the philosopher. We said somewhere, that they must be judged by the reason, didn't we? But reasoning is chiefly the facility of the philosopher.

'If then that which is to be determined was best determined by riches and gain, which the mercenary man commended, or despised like the Stoic, wouldn't that, of necessity, be the most agreeable to truth. And if through honour, victory and bravery, mustn't it be as the ambitious and contentious man determined? But since it is determined by experience, and prudence, and reason, that which the philosopher and the lover of reason commends must be the most true. Of the three pleasures, then, that is the most pleasant which belongs to that part of the soul by which we learn the most, and he among us, in whom this part governs, lives the most pleasant life.' 'How can it be otherwise? For the wise man, having the full right to commend, commends his own life.' 'But which life, does our judge pronounce the second pleasure?' 'It is clear, that of the warlike and ambitious; for this is nearer to his own disposition than that of the lucrative. And that of the covetous is last of all.

'In these two cases, the one after the other, the just man has twice overcome the unjust. The third victory now, as at the Olympic Games, is sacred to Olympian Zeus, the Saviour. For consider that the pleasure of the others is not in every way genuine, but that of the wise man's is. Neither are they pure, but merely a kind of outline of purity, as I think I have heard it once said, by one of the wisest of men. And this truly would be the greatest and most complete downfall of the unjust. Tell me; don't we say that pain is opposite to pleasure and don't we say that there is such a possibility as to neither feel pleasure or pain? That being in the middle of both these sensations, it is a certain tranquillity of the soul that refers to them. Do you remember the speeches of the diseased, which they utter in their sicknesses? How nothing is more pleasant than good health, but that it escaped their notice before they became very ill, that it was the most pleasant.

'And are you not aware of hearing those who are suffering any acute pain say that there is nothing more pleasant than cessation from pain? And you may notice in men, I imagine, the same exclamations, when they are in many other similar circumstances. Where, when in pain, they extol the freedom from pain, and the tranquillity of such a state, as being the most pleasant, yet do not extol that of feeling joy. And when anyone ceases to feel joy, this absence of pleasure will be painful. But can what is neither become both? And surely at least, when any pleasant sensation or any painful sensation is in the soul, both sensations are in a certain movement. But didn't that which is neither painful nor pleasant appear just now to be tranquillity, and in the middle of these two? How is it right to think it is pleasant not to be in pain, or painful not to enjoy pleasure?

'In these cases, tranquillity is not really so, but it appears pleasant in contrast with the painful, and painful in contrast with the pleasant. And there is nothing genuine to be known in these appearances as to the truth of pleasure, but a certain mental delusion. Consider the pleasures which do not arise from the cessation of pains, this you may not necessarily infer from the present discourse, that these two naturally coexist. It is that pleasure which is the cessation of pain, and pain is the cessation of pleasure. Let us consider the pleasures from the sense of smell. For these pleasures, without any preceding pain, are all of a sudden quite strong, and when they end, they leave no pain behind them. Let us not be over-persuaded that pure pleasure is merely the removal of pain, or pain is simply the removal of pleasure.

'But yet those sensations which extend through the body to the soul, and which are called pleasures, the greatest part of them, and the most frequent, are of this kind, certain cessations of pain. And are not the preconceptions of pleasure and pain, which arise in the mind from the expectation of these sensations of the same kind? Do you know then, of what kind they consist, and what they chiefly resemble?' 'What do they consist of and resemble, Socrates?' 'Do you think,' said I, 'there is any such phenomenon in nature as this, above, below, and in the middle? Do you think that anyone, when he is brought from the below up to the middle, imagines anything other than that he is brought to the above? And when he stands in the middle, and looks down from where he was brought up, will he imagine he is anywhere else than above, while yet he has never seen the real above?

'But if he should be carried back again, he would conjecture he was carried down to the below, and would conjecture according to the truth. Would he not be affected in all these respects, from his not having had any experience in what is really above, and in the middle, and below? Would you wonder then, that while men are inexperienced in the truth, besides having unsound opinions about most other things, they are likewise affected in this same way as to pleasure and pain, and what is between them? So that, even when they are brought to experience what is painful, they imagine truly, and are truly pained; but when from pain they are brought to the middle, they strongly imagine that they have arrived at the fullness of pleasure. In the same way as those who along with the black colour look at the grey, through inexperience of the white are deceived. So, those who consider pain along with a freedom from pain, are deceived through inexperience of pleasure.

'But consider it in this way. Are not hunger and thirst, and such like, certain feelings of emptiness and need to be experienced in the stomach? And are not ignorance and folly a feeling of emptiness in the intuition of the soul? And is not the stomach filled when it receives food, and the soul when it receives understanding? But which is the more real feeling of fulfilment, and that of the less, in the experience of Real Being?' 'It is obvious, the more real feeling of fulfilment appertains to the soul.' 'Which classes, do you think, experience most knowledge of pure essence or existence? Whether these be those which participate of bread, drink, and meat, and all such kinds of nourishment, or that class which participates in true philosophy, science, and understanding, in short, of all virtue?'

'But judge it in this way. That which adheres to what is immutable, and immortal, and true, is so in itself, does it therefore seem to you to have more of the reality of Being, than that which adheres to what is mutable, and is mortal, in itself, and is therefore in a class of this kind?' 'This latter differs very much from that which is immutable, Socrates, while the former agrees.' 'Does the essence of that which is mutable sustain more of essence or existence than that of science?' 'By no means, if you regard science as immutable.' 'But what with relation to truth?' 'Not this either.' 'If science sustains less of the truth, does it not also do so regarding essence? In short, do not the regularities relating to the care of the body participate less of truth and essence, than those relating to the care of the soul? And the same could be said of the body compared with the soul.

'Is not that which is filled with more Real Being, and is itself a more Real Being, in reality more truly filled, than that which is filled with less Real Being, and is itself a less Real Being? If it is pleasant to be filled with what is suitable to nature, that which is filled is, in reality, more Real Being, and must be both more real, and more likely to enjoy essential pleasure. But that which participates of less Real Being, must be less truly and firmly filled, and participates of a more uncertain and less genuine pleasure. Those who are unacquainted with wisdom and virtue, and are mainly concerned with feasting and similar diversions, are carried it seems to the below, and back again to the middle, and there they wander for lifetimes. But, never passing beyond that condition, they never look towards what is the true above, nor are they carried to it, nor are they ever really filled with the experience of Real Being, nor have they ever tasted pure pleasure!

'But, after the manner of brutes, they are always looking downwards, bowing down towards the solid Earth and their dining tables, they live feeding and coupling. And from a lust for these diversions, kicking and pushing at one another with iron horns and hoofs. They kill one another through their insatiableness, as those who are filling themselves with unreal Being and never know Real Beingness, so they are unfriendly even to themselves.' 'You are, Socrates, just like an intellectual boxer, punching us to accept your truth, and then finishing your discourse perfectly with a knock-out blow, like an oracle,' said Glauco, 'who declaims on the sensual life of the multitude.' 'Thank you, Glauco, I will now deliver the knock-out blow!

'Must they not, of necessity, be conversant with pleasure mixed with pains, images of the true pleasure, only sketched in outline, and coloured by their juxtapositions, one beside the other? So, both their pleasures and pains will appear vehement and engender mad passions in the foolish. Also they must tend to fight about these things, as Stesichorus says about those at Troy who fought over the image of Helen, through ignorance of the true Helen. And what about the spirited part of the soul? Must not other similar phenomena happen, whenever anyone gratifies that faculty, either in the way of envy, through ambition, or in the way of violence, through contentiousness, or in the way of anger, through moroseness? Always pursuing a glut of honour, conquest, and anger, both without reason, and without intelligence?

'What then, shall we boldly say concerning all the varied pleasures, contrasting the avaricious and the ambitious, with those who are obedient to science and reason, and, in conjunction with these, pursue and obtain the genuine pleasure of which the prudent part of the soul is the leader? They shall surely obtain the truest pleasures, as far as it is possible for them to attain true pleasure, and in so much as they follow truth and pleasures which are properly their own, since what is best for everyone, must be most properly his own! When the whole soul is obedient to the philosophic tendency, and there is no sedition contained in it, then every part of the soul, in every other respect, performs its proper function, and is just, and also enjoys its own pleasures, such as are of the best, and as far as is possible the most true.

'But, wise Adimantus, when any of the other lower faculties govern, it happens that the soul neither attains its own pleasures, and it compels the other parts to pursue a pleasure foreign to them, and is false. Do not the parts of the soul which are the most remote from true philosophy and pure reason especially accomplish such things? And is not that which is most remote from law and order, also most remote from reason? And do not the amorous and the Tyrannical desires appear to be most remote from law and order, and the Aristocratic and moderate ones, the least remote? The Tyrant, I think, is the most remote from true pleasure, and so is most probably his own essence, and the philosophical man shall be the closest. And the Tyrant shall lead a most unpleasant life, and the Philosopher King or Guardian, the most pleasant.

'Do you know then, how much more unpleasant a life the Tyrant leads than the Philosopher King or Guardian? There are three pleasures, it seems, one genuine, and two illegitimate. The Tyrant, in carrying the illegitimate to extremity, and flying from law and reason, dwells with slavish pleasures as his life-guards, and how far he is inferior, is not even easily to be said, unless it is done in this way. The Tyrannical character is somehow the third step from the Oligarchic character, and the Democratic is in the middle between them. Does he not live with the third kind of pleasure, far distant from him with reference to truth, if our former reasoning be correct? But the Oligarchic is the third step from the Regal, if we suppose the Aristocratic and the Regal to be much the same.

'The Tyrant then, is remote from true pleasure, thrice three times. A plain surface may be a good image of Tyrannical pleasure, to use a geometric metaphor. But if we take the second and third increase of steps away from him, it is obvious how great a distance he is from Real Being. If now, conversely, shall we say that the Philosopher King is distant from the Tyrant as to truth from overindulgent pleasure. Shall the Philosopher King or Guardian, on completing this metaphorical multiplication, find him leading the most pleasantly blissful life, and the Tyrant the most miserable and wretched one 729 times, I reckon [laughter]?' 'You have heaped up a prodigious amount of difference between these two men, Socrates, the just and the unjust, with reference to pleasure and pain.' 'If then the good and just man surpasses so far the evil and unjust man in extravagant pleasures, in what a prodigious degree further shall he surpass him in the majesty of life, in beauty and in virtue!

BOOK 10

POETRY AND PHILOSOPHY

'I observe,' I said, 'for very many reasons, that we have established our city in the right manner, beyond all question, and I am most surely convinced of it when I remember the rules respecting poetry. That no part of it which is imitative should by any means be admitted. For it appears, now most of all, that it is not to be admitted, since the several forms of the soul have been distinguished from one another. That I may tell it to you, I trust you will not accuse me before the composers of tragedy, and the rest of the imitative kind of dramatists, for all such as these seem to be the ruin of the mind of the hearers; that is, those who haven't the facility to enable them to discern their own true nature.

'It must be said, although admitting a certain friendship and reverence for dear old Homer, which I have held from my childhood, and which restrains me somewhat from telling you what I now feel. For he seems both to have been the first teacher and leader of all these good composers of tragedy, but even such a great poet must not be counted upon to understand the truth. And what I mean by that must necessarily be said.' 'Can you tell me first, Socrates, what you mean by imitation in the poetic sense? For I myself don't understand it fully.' 'Certainly. Are you willing then, that we begin our enquiry by our usual method?'

'Let us suppose, for example, there are many beds and tables, and the ideas that spring to mind, when regarding these pieces of furniture, are two, one of bed, and one of table. And are we not inclined to say that the workmen who made each of these pieces of furniture, looked towards these ideas, the one of bed, and the other of table, which we all use, and all other articles he makes, in the same way? For not one of the craftsmen makes the idea itself, how can he? But now, see how I describe another workman? One who can make all things, as each manual artificer does. A skilful and wonderful workman I speak about, for this same great artificer is not only able to make all sorts of utensils, but he can also make everything which springs from the Earth, and he carves or moulds all sorts of animals and men himself, and besides these creatures, he makes the Earth, and the heavens, and the Gods, and all things in heaven, and in Hades under the Earth.' 'You speak of a perfectly wonderful sophist, Socrates.'

'Ha, ha, you do not believe me; does it seem to you that there is no such artist? Or, that he is the maker of all things, and in another way he is not? Or do you not perceive that even you yourself might be able to make all these things, in a certain manner? It is not difficult, but is performed in many ways, and quickly, but in fact I will tell you the quickest way of all. If you choose to take a mirror, and carry it around everywhere, then you will quickly make the Sun, and the stars in the heavens, the Earth, yourself, the other animals, utensils, vegetables, and all that we have now mentioned.' 'Yes, the reflected appearances, but not the real things.'

'You speak well with that remark. But you will come to see, I think, that even the painter does not make what he paints, although the painter too, in a certain manner, at least, can make a bed, can he not? But with reference to the bed-maker, did we not agree that he does not make the form which we say exists, which is the idea of bed, but only a particular bed? For if he does not make that which *is*, he does not make Real Being, but something which only imitates Real Being, not Real Being itself. And furthermore if anyone should say that the work of a bed-maker, or of any other handicraftsman, was Real Beingness, he wouldn't seem to speak the truth. Are now you willing, that, with reference to this very question, we enquire concerning the imitator, and who he really is?

'Are there not then these three types of beds? One which exists in nature, say of leaves or moss for example, and which we might say, God made; and one which the joiner makes, and one which the painter makes. Now, the painter, the bed-maker, and God, these three preside over three types of beds. But God, whether because He was not willing, or whether there was some necessity for it, that He should not make just one bed in nature, made this one only, which is truly a bed; but two, exactly the same, have never been produced by God, nor ever will be produced by Him. Because, if He had made two, again one would have appeared, the form of which both these two would have possessed, and that form would be that which is Real Bedness, and not the other, which is an imitation. God then, knowing this, and willing to be the maker of Bedness, and really existing, but not any particular kind of bed, nor to be any particular bed-maker, produced what was in its nature one.

'Are you willing that we call Him the natural creator of this idea, or something of this nature?' 'It is just so, since He has, in His nature, made both this and all other things.' 'But what about the joiner? Is he not the maker of a bed? And the painter, too, the workman, and any maker of such a work? But what will you say that he is in relation to the bed?' 'This, it seems to me, we may most reasonably call him, the imitator of what these other are the workmen of in their manufacture.' 'So be it, you call him then the imitator who makes what is generated as the third from nature? And this man, the composer of tragedy shall be called likewise, since he is an imitator, a sort of third, sprung from the Almighty King and the Truth; and in a like manner are all the other imitators.

'We agreed, then, as to the nature of the imitator; but tell me this, concerning the painter, whether you think he undertakes to imitate each essential thing in nature, or the works of artisans in relation to things?' 'The works of artisans.' 'Whether such as they really are, or such as they appear to be? To determine this further, does a bed differ anything from itself, whether he views it obliquely, or directly opposite, or from any particular position? Or, does it differ in no particular way, but only appears different, and in the same way as all other things when moved around? Consider this too, with reference to which of the two is painting directed in each particular work; whether with reference to Real Essential Being, or merely to imitate it as it appears, and whether this is only the appearance, or an imitation of truth?' 'Of appearance, surely.'

'The imitative art, then, is far from the truth, and on this account, it seems, he is able to paint these things, because he is able to attain to some small part of each particular, and that is but an image. Thus we say that a painter will paint us a shoemaker, a joiner, and other artisans, although he is unskilled in these crafts. Yet he will be able to deceive children and ignorant people, if he is a good painter. Even when he paints a joiner, and shows him at a distance, so far away as to make them imagine he is a real joiner. And this, I think, my friend, we must consider with reference to all these things, that when anyone tells us of such a painter, that he has met with a man who is skilled in all manner of workmanship, and everything else, which several artists understand, and that there is nothing which he does not know more accurately than any other person. We ought to reply to such a questioner, that he is a simple man, and that it seems, like one whom having met with some magician and mimic, he has been deceived; and that it has seemed to him, that he knows everything. This misjudgement springs from his own innate incapacity to distinguish between real knowledge and ignorance, or between reality and imitation.

'Should we not then, in the next place, consider tragedy, and its prime leader, the great poet, Homer? Since, we hear from some, that these poets understand all the arts, and all human affairs, in respect of virtue and vice, as well as all divine manifestations. For, a good poet must necessarily compose with knowledge, if he means to compose well. It impels us, then, to consider whether those who have met with these imitators have been deceived and, on hearing their works, have not perceived that they are in the third distant place from Real Being, and that their works are such and can easily be made by one who doesn't even realize the truth. Thus they make poems about phantasms, and not Real Being. And we must ask, whether they do say something to any real purpose, and whether the good poets in reality have knowledge of those truths which they seem, to the multitude, to express with elegance.

'Do you think then, that if anyone were able to make both of these, that which is imitated, and likewise the image, he would allow himself seriously to apply to the workmanship of the images, and propose this to himself as the best thing in life? If he were, in reality, intelligent in these things which he imitates, he would go further and seriously apply himself to the real rather than to the imitations, and would endeavour to leave behind him many beautiful works, as monuments of himself, and would study rather to be himself the person commended, than the imitator.' 'I think so, for neither is the honour, nor the Good, to be earned in the same way.'

'As to ordinary matters, let us not call them to account, asking Homer or any other of the poets, whether any of them is in any way skilled in medicine, and not just an imitator of medical discourses. For which of the ancient or later poets can be said to have restored any to health, as Asclepius did? Or what students in medicine have left behind them medical knowledge, as he left to his descendants? We shall not ask them concerning the other arts, but dismiss them. But with reference to those great and most glorious adventures which Homer attempts to write about, concerning battles and armies, constitutions of cities, and the education most suitable for men and women, it is just, somehow, to question him, while we demand more epic poetry from him. So, friend Homer, if you are not the third from the truth with regard to virtue, being the workman of an image, which we have defined an imitator to be, but the second, and are able to discern which pursuits render men better or worse, both in private and public, tell us please, which of the cities has been better constituted by you, as Lacedæmon was by Lycurgus, and many other great and small cities by many others. And what city acknowledges you to have been a good lawgiver, and to have been of advantage to them.

'Italy and Sicily acknowledge Charondas and we Athenians

acknowledge Solon, but will anyone acknowledge you?' 'I do not think so,' said Glauco. 'It is never even claimed by the Homerids themselves.' 'But what war in Homer's day is recorded to have been well conducted by him as leader, or counsellor? Not one. But what are his discoveries? For among the works of a wise man there are many discoveries and inventions spoken about, with respect to the arts, and other affairs, such as those of Thales the Milesian, and Anacharsis the Scythian. By no means is there any such event recorded, in the public domain, whereby Homer has said to have served as a private tutor to any who delighted in his conversation, or has delivered down to posterity a certain Homeric manner of life?

'This is in contrast with Pythagoras, who was remarkably beloved on this account, and, even to this day, many follow the Pythagoræan manner of life, and consequently appear to be somehow more eminent, well beyond others in wisdom.' 'There is nothing of this kind said about Homer. For Creophylus, the companion of Homer, appears more ridiculous still in his education, than in his name, if what is said of Homer be true. For, it is said that he was greatly neglected when he lived under Homer's tuition.' 'So it is rumoured; but do you think, Glauco, that if Homer had been able to educate men, and to render them better, as being capable not only to imitate in verse in most matters, and to understand them, would he not then have attracted many companions, and have been honoured and beloved by them? For Protagoras the Abderite, and Prodicus the Chian, and many others, were able to persuade the men of their times, conversing with them privately, that they will neither be able to govern their family, nor their city, unless they themselves, preside over their education. And for this tuition of theirs, they are so exceedingly beloved, that their companions almost carry them about on their heads.

'Would then the men of Homer's time have left him or Hesiod to go about singing their songs, if he had been able to educate men in the ways of virtue, and then retain him with gold, and oblige him to stay with them? Or, if they could not persuade him, would they not as scholars have followed him everywhere, until they had obtained sufficient education? Shall we not then establish this point, that all the poets, beginning with Homer, are imitators of the images of virtue, and of other subjects, about which they compose, but that they do not attain to the truth. And as we have just said, a painter who himself knows nothing about the making of shoes, will paint a shoemaker, who shall appear to be real, in the eyes of those who are unintelligent, but who view only according to the colour and the figure?

'In the same way, I think, we shall say that the poet colours over with his names and words, certain tones and shades of the several arts, while he understands nothing himself. But he merely imitates, so others such as himself, who, reading descriptions in his compositions, imagine he has great knowledge. And if he says anything about shoemaking in metre, rhyme and harmony, he seems to speak perfectly well, and similarly with a military expedition, or anything else; so great an enchantment have these epic spectacles. As you know, in what way poetical topics appear when stripped of musical colouring, and expressed apart by themselves, for you have somewhere seen them. Don't they resemble the faces of people who are in their prime, but who are not as truly beautiful as they were before their youthful bloom forsook them?' 'A good metaphor Socrates, quite poetic [laughter].'

'Come now, let's look at this. The maker of the image, whom we shall call the imitator, knows nothing of Real Being, but only that which is apparent. Let us not leave it there, just expressed by halves, but let us wholly perceive it. A painter, we say, will paint reins, and a bridle. And the leather-cutter, and the smith, will make them. Does the painter understand what kind of reins and bridle these ought to be, or not? Even the smith and the leather-cutter, do not know. But he who knows how to use them is the horseman alone. Shall we not agree it is so in everything else with reference to each particular work, that there are these three arts? First, that skill by which to use it, that which is to make it, and that which is to imitate it.

'Are then the virtues, and the beauties, and the rectitude inherent in every creation, animal, human being, and deed, useful for nothing else, than for the use for which each particular object was made, or created? Then, he who makes use of each particular object must be most skilful, and be able to tell the manufacturer whether what he makes is good or bad, with reference to its use, when he uses it. So, for example, a player on the pipe tells the pipe-maker concerning pipes, what necessary accoutrements are of service in pipe playing, and he will give orders how he should make them, but the workman does not do so. Does not the pipe player, being knowledgeable, pronounce on good and bad pipes, and then the pipe-maker, believing him, makes pipes accordingly?

'With reference then to one and the same instrument, the maker shall have the right opinion concerning its beauty or deformity, whilst he is conversant with one who is knowledgeable, and he is obliged to hear from him, but he who uses it, only has that actual knowledge. But whether the imitator has any knowledge about using the object he paints, whether they are suitable and adequate, or otherwise, is an open question? Or does he have a right opinion from his very Being which is necessarily conversant with the knowledgeable, and thus intuitively is encouraged in what way he should paint? So the imitator then has neither correct, direct knowledge, nor right opinion about what he imitates with reference to beauty or deformity.

'The imitator then would be ignorant in his imitation concerning what he paints. But, he will imitate, at least, without knowing whether each particular detail is bad or good. But it is most likely that he will imitate in such a way as appears to be beautiful to the multitude, and those who know nothing. We have now, indeed, sufficiently, it seems, settled these questions, that the imitator knows nothing worth mentioning about those things which he imitates, but that imitation is a kind of amusement, and not a serious affair. And likewise those who compose tragedies and comedies in iambics, alexandrines and heroics, are all imitators to the highest degree. In this way, every kind of disturbance is created within the soul. And this is the weakness of the human mind on which the art of conjuring and of deceiving by light and shade, metre and figures of speech, and other ingenious devices imposes, having an effect on us like magic.

'Then, in heaven's name, this imitation of Real Being is somehow in the third degree away from the truth! To what part, then, of man does it belong, having the power it possesses? The same magnitude perceived by sight, does not appear in the same manner when near, and when at a distance. And the same sticks will appear crooked and straight, when we look at them in water, and different again when out of water; either concave or convex, through the error of sight. And it is the same with colours according to the light. And have not the arts of measuring, numbering, and weighing seemed to me most ingenious aids in fashioning these apparitions? Thus that the apparent, greater or less; the apparent, lighter or heavier, may not govern us, but only the *principle* which has been numbered, measured, and weighed? But this is, at least, the work of the rational part in the soul.

'But while reason often measures and declares some things to be greater or smaller than other things, or equal; the contrary happens with reference to these arts. But did we not say that it was impossible for the same person to have contrary opinions about the same things at the same time? And so far we have said rightly. That rational part of the soul, then, which judges contrary to measurement and numbering, would not seem to be the same as that part which judges according to measurement and numbering. But surely, at least, that which we trust to measure and to compute would seem to be the best part of the soul. That, then, which opposes this, will be one of the depraved parts of us. It was this then that I wished we should be agreed upon, when I said that painting and poetry, and in short imitation, being far from the truth, delights in its own work, conversing with that part in us which is far from wisdom, and is not a companion and friend to any sound or genuine purpose.

'Imitation then, being depraved in itself, and combining with that which is depraved, generates depraved consequences; whether this is the case with reference to the imitation which is by sight only, or likewise so with reference to that by hearing or reading, which we call poetry. But, let us not trust to the likelihood suggested by painting, but proceed to the consideration of that part of the mind with which the imitation through poetry is conversant, and see whether it is depraved or worthy.

'Let us proceed then in this way. Poetic imitation, we say, imitates men who act either voluntarily or involuntarily; and who from the result of their actions imagine that they have done either well or badly, and in all these cases gain either pain or pleasure. Does it do any more than this? In all this, does the man agree with himself or, as he disagreed with reference to sight, and had contrary opinions within himself of the same things, at one and the same time? Does he, in the same way, disagree likewise in his actions, and struggle with himself? But I recollect that this is not the occasion for us to settle this matter any further. For, in our reasoning, we have already sufficiently determined all these principles, that our soul is full of a thousand such contraries existing in it.

'But it seems to me necessary to discuss now, what was then omitted. We said formerly that a good man, when he meets with a disaster such as the loss of a son, or of anything else which he values the most of all, he will bear it, of all men, the easiest, like the Stoics. But let us now consider this further. Will he ever grieve again at all, or is this impossible? Or will he, however, moderate his grief?' 'The truth is rather this last statement.' 'But tell me this, regarding him, whether he will struggle more with grief and oppose it, when he is observed by his equals, or when he is in solitude, alone by himself?' 'Much more when he is observed.' 'But when he is alone, he will venture to say many things, which, if anyone heard him, he would be ashamed of, and he will do many things which he would not wish anyone to see him doing. Is it not, then, reason and law which command him to restrain his grief, and what drags him to grief is the passion itself?

'As there is in each man or woman, an opposite tendency with regard to the same tendency, at one and the same time; so we must necessarily say that he has two conductors of his behaviour. And shall we also say that one of them is always ready to obey the law wherever the law leads him? Law, in a certain way, says that it is best in misfortunes to have the greatest tranquillity possible, and not to bear any ill feeling to the Gods. Since the good and evil in such events as these is not disclosed, and no advantage follows the bearing of ill fortune, as nothing in human affairs is worthy of great concern. Because it is destined to happen, is not entirely in our hands and control. Besides, grief proves a hindrance to the nobility inherent in them, which we ought to have always with us.

'To deliberate on the event; then as with a throw of the dice, to regulate his affairs according to what destiny casts; and, in whatever way events turn out, reason shall declare that all happens for the best! To accept all as the best, not as children when they fall, to lie still, and waste their time in crying, but always to accustom the soul to apply in the speediest manner great wisdom, to heal and rectify what has happened, dismissing lamentation as a leaf falls from the tree. We cannot understand the divine wisdom that controls events with our petty minds. One should, thus, behave in the best possible manner in every situation, fearlessly. And didn't we say that the best way is to be willing to follow that which is most rational? And shall we also say that the part of the mind which leads to the memory of the affliction, is prone to wailing, and is insatiably given over to such self-indulgence, is irrational, perverse, and a friend of cowardice?

'Isn't then the grieving tendency that part of the mind which permits a great deal of varied imitation as its guest?

But the prudent and tranquil part of the soul, which is always uniform with itself, is not easily affected by imitation. A spiritual disposition is foreign to such influences. It is plain, then, that the imitative poet or rhapsodist, when disclaiming, is not intended for such an august part of the soul as this. Neither are their skills fitted to achieve such an influence, if they mean to gain the approval of the multitude. But the poet can reach the passionate and multiform part of the soul, as it is easily subject to imitation.

'May we not then, with justice, take hold of the imitative poet, and place him, as corresponding with the painter? For he resembles him, because, in truth, he affects depravity. And in this too he resembles him, in being conversant with a different part of the soul from that which is the best part. And so we may, with justice, not admit him into our city which is to be well regulated, because he excites and nourishes this lower part of the soul, and, by strengthening it, undermines the rational part. And as he who in a city makes the wicked powerful, betrays the city, and destroys the best men, in the same manner we shall say that the imitative poet establishes a bad state in the soul of each individual, gratifying the foolish part of it, which neither discerns what is great, nor what is little. But it will believe the same things are sometimes great and sometimes petty, forming little images in its own imagination, altogether remote from truth.

'But we have not as yet brought the greatest accusation against imitative verse, that is, somehow, a very dreadful one, that it is able to corrupt even the good. How could it not, since it acts in this manner? So listen, and consider, for somehow, even with the best of us, when we hear Homer, or any of the tragic writers, imitating some of the heroes when in grief, pouring forth long speeches in sorrow, bewailing and beating their breasts, you know that we are delighted. Then yielding ourselves, we follow along; and, sympathizing with them, seriously commend him as an able poet, and whoever else affects us in this manner. I know it myself. But when any domestic grief befalls any of us, you perceive, on the other hand, that we ennoble ourselves with the opposite behaviour, if we can be quiet, and endure; this keeping quiet, being the better part of a virtuous man or woman.

'But, if you consider that the better part of us which, in our private misfortunes, we forcibly restrain, and we keep from weeping and wailing, although by nature, desiring to give way to these obsessions; that is the very part which the imitative poets fill and gratify. And that part in us, which is naturally the best, being not sufficiently instructed, either by reason or habit, grows remiss in its Guardianship, by over-attending to the sufferings of others. For he believes it is in no way disgraceful to commend and pity one who grieves immoderately, whilst he professes to be an enlightened man or woman. By this, he or she gains a vicarious pleasure, which it would not choose to be deprived of, by despising the whole of the imitative poem. For, I think, it falls to the care of a few of us, to be able to consider that what we feel with respect to the fortunes of others must necessarily be felt with respect to our own; since it is not easy for a man to bear up under his own misfortunes, who strongly cherishes the bewailing disposition over the misfortunes of others. ·

'And is not our reasoning the same with reference to the ridiculous? For when you hear, in imitation, at a tragedy or comedy, or in private conversation, what you would be ashamed to do yourself, in order to excite laughter, and are delighted with it, and imitate it, you commit the same sin as in the tragedy or comedy. For that ludicrous part of the soul, which, when it wanted to engage in foolish laughter, was formerly restrained by reason from a fear of gaining a reputation for scornfulness; but now letting itself loose, and allowing itself to grow vigorously, you are often imperceptibly brought, by your own behaviour, to be a buffoon.

'And the case is even more so with excessive venereal pleasures, anger, and the whole of the passions; as well as with the sorrowful or the joyful. All these, as we have said, may betray us in every action. The poetical imitation of these excesses has the same effect upon us, for they feed and water those tendencies which should be parched. It then rules as our governor of those tendencies which should really be governed by the better part of the soul, in order for us to become much better and happier, instead of being sadder and more miserable.

'Therefore, my dear Glauco, when you meet with the admirers of Homer, who tell you how this poet instructed Greece, and that he deserves to be taken as a master to teach a man both the management and the knowledge of human affairs; and that a man should regulate the whole of his life according to this poet; we should indeed love and embrace such people, as being the best, as they are able, and agree with them that Homer is most poetical, and the first of tragic writers. But they must know full well, that beautiful, truly poetic hymns to the Gods, and the praises of worthy actions, are alone to be admitted into our ideal city.

'But if we should admit the imitative pleasurable muse, in song, or verse, you will have pleasure and pain reigning in the city; instead of law, and that higher reason, which is always the best for the community. Let these opinions now, be our apologia, when we recollect that what we have said with reference to imitative, but not religious poetry, which we very properly dismissed from our ideal republic, as it is now described, as higher reason obliges us. And furthermore, unless we are to be accused of a certain roughness, and rusticity, we must acknowledge that there is an ancient tradition stating the variance between philosophy and poetry. For example, such verses as these: *That bawling bitch, which at his master barks*; and *He's great in empty eloquence of fools*; and *The mob of heads too wise*; and *On trifles still they plod, because they're poor*; and a thousand such like verses, are marks of an ancient opposition between true philosophy, the queen of the sciences, and adulterated, prostituted poetry, no matter how talented the imitator!

'But nevertheless, let it be said, that if anyone can assign a really good reason why the poetry and the imitation which are calculated for pleasure ought to be permitted in a well regulated city, we, for our part, will gladly admit them, as we are at least honest with ourselves, that we are often charmed by them. But to betray what appears to be truth is unholy. For are not you, my friends, charmed by this imitation, and most especially when you see it performed by Homer? So, Glauco, is it not just then, that we introduce higher religious poetry, either in song, or in any other measure? And we may at least grant, to its defenders, who are not generally adulterous poets, but true lovers of devotional poetry, to speak up on its behalf, and show that it is not only pleasant, but profitable for republics, and for human life. And then we shall listen with pleasure, for we shall gain a great deal from it, when it shall seem to be not only pleasant but also profitable.'

'How is it possible we should not gain by religious poetry?'

he asked. 'If it happens, otherwise, my friend, we shall do as those who have been in love when they discover their love is unprofitable, they desist. So we in like manner, through this love of higher poetry that prevails in our best republics, we shall be well pleased to see it performed as the best and the truest, and we shall hear it until it needs no further defence. So we shall take along with us this discourse which we have held, as a counter charm, and incantation, being afraid to fall back again into a childish and vulgar love of prostituted poetry. We shall listen then, convinced that we are not to be applauding such poetry as this, as if it is a serious affair, and a valuable approach to the truth. For, dear friend Glauco, mighty is the contest, and not just as it seems, only to struggle to become a good man rather than a bad man, but not to be moved, either through honour, riches, magistracy, or poetic imitation, ever to neglect justice, and the other virtues.

'But we have not yet discussed the greatest prize of virtue, and the rewards laid up for her. For what else is there, that can be so great in such a short time? All this period from infancy to old age is but little in respect of the whole of the soul's existence. Do you think that an immortal being ought to be much more concerned about such a trivial period as one life time, and not about the whole of eternity?' 'I think,' he said, 'about eternity.' 'Have you not perceived,' I replied, 'that our soul is immortal, and never perishes?' On which he, looking at me and wondering, said, 'By heavens, no I have not fully, no indeed! But are you able to demonstrate this logically?' 'I should otherwise act unjustly if I could not, and I think you yourself can demonstrate it, for it is in no respect difficult.

'You shall hear then, so pay attention well, Glauco and the

rest of you! Now, is there not something, which you call the Good, and something which you call evil? Do you then conceive them in the same manner as I do? That which destroys and corrupts everything is the evil, and that which preserves and benefits everything is the Good. Do you not also say there is something which is good, and something which is bad in each particular case, when you need to make a moral judgement? For example, when blindness strikes the eyes, disease infects the body, the failure of harvests, the rotting of wood, the rusting of metal; and almost everything has its connate evil and corruption? And when anything of this kind strikes any other thing, does it not render that which it strikes as corrupt, and in the end dissolves and destroys it? Its very name usually signifies evil, and the consequent corruption destroys each particular thing on which it falls. For, if this doesn't destroy it, nothing else will destroy it. For that which is good will never destroy anything which is pure and uncorrupted.

'If, then, we shall be able to find, among human beings, anyone who has no evil in him or her which renders them corrupt, and is unable to dissolve and destroy it, shall we not then know that a being that is so constituted cannot easily be destroyed? Is there not some force which renders the soul evil? All these things which we have now mentioned, injustice, intemperance, cowardice, ignorance, and so on, are examples. But does any of these corruptions dissolve and destroy it? Attend now, that we may not be imposed on, by thinking that an unjust and foolish man, when he is detected acting unjustly, is then destroyed through his injustice, which is the corruption of his soul. But consider it like this. As disease, which is the corruption of the animal body, dissolves and destroys that body, and reduces it, so it is no longer a body, but a corpse; then, so all those forces we have mentioned, being destroyed by their own evil, inherent in them, and possessing them, are reduced to nonexistence.

'Consider now the soul in the same manner. Does injustice, or any other vice, possessing it, then by possessing and adhering to it, corrupt and deface it, until, bringing it to death, it separates itself from the body? Consider this, Glauco, that neither by the corruption of meats, whether they be full of mouldiness, or rottenness, or whatever else, do we imagine our body can be destroyed. But if this corruption in them creates in the body a disease of the body, we will say that, through their means, the body is destroyed by its own evil, which is the disease. But we will never allow that by the corruption of food, which is one thing, and the body, which is another thing, can ever by this foreign evil, without creating in it its own peculiar evil, and be at any time destroyed.

'According to the same reasoning, then, unless the corruption of the body creates a corruption of the soul, let us never permit that the soul can be destroyed by an evil which is foreign to it, without its own peculiar evil; one evil being the cause of another evil. Let us either refute these arguments as inadequate reasoning. For, so long as they remain unrefuted, let us at no time say that the soul shall ever in any degree be destroyed, either by burning fever, by any other disease, or by slaughter; even though a man should cut the whole body into the smallest pieces possible. And we will never allow it to be said, that when a foreign evil befalls anything, whilst its own inherent evil is not within it, neither the soul nor anything else can be destroyed.' 'But this,' he said, 'no one can ever show, that the souls of those who die are rendered more unjust by death.'

'But if anyone,' I replied, 'shall dare to contend with us in reasoning that he does not admit that souls are immortal, I would say that if he says that when a man dies he may become more wicked and unjust, we shall ask him to prove to us that he tells the truth in telling us that injustice is deadly to the soul as is a disease. And that those who embrace it are destroyed by it as by a disease, destructive in its own nature, and those most speedily who embrace it most, and those less slowly who embrace it least. And not as at present, where the unjust die having this punishment inflicted on them by others.' 'By heaven,' he said, 'injustice would not appear perfectly dreadful, if it was not deadly to him who practises it, and that it is a deliverance from evil. But I rather think it will appear to be altogether the reverse, destroying others as far as it can, but rendering the unjust extremely alive, and, in conjunction with being alive, wakeful!.'

'You say well, Glauco, for, when a man's own wickedness and peculiar evil is insufficient to kill and destroy the soul, hardly can that evil, which aims at the destruction of another, destroy a soul, or anything else but that which it is aimed against. Since it is destroyed by no particular evil, either peculiar or foreign, is it not plain that, through necessity, it always exists? And, if it always exists, it is immortal. Let us then be certain in this matter. And if it be so, you will perceive that the same souls will always remain, for their number will never become less, none of them ever being destroyed, nor will they become greater. For if the number of immortals was created to be greater, you know it would subtract from the mortal, and in the end all would be immortal. But let us not, think that this will be the case, for reason will not allow it, as the soul in its truest nature is of such a kind as to be full of much variety, dissimilitude, and difference. That cannot easily become eternal when it is compounded of so many things, and which hasn't the most beautiful composition, as has now seemed to us, to be the case with the soul.

'The pure, just soul then, is immortal, both confirmed by our present reasoning, and in others' reasoning too, which obliges us to accept that this is true. But, in order to know the kind of Being the soul is, in truth, one should not try to contemplate it, as it is damaged, both by its conjunction with the body, and by other evils, as we now know. But such as it is when it becomes purified, then it must by reasoning be fully contemplated. And he who does this, will find it far more beautiful, and will more plainly see through justice, and injustice, and everything which we have now discussed. But now we have told the truth concerning this question, such as appears to us at present.

'We have seen it, indeed, in the same condition in which they see the shipwrecked body, Glauco, where they cannot easily perceive his original nature, because the limbs of his body are partly broken, and others are torn away. And he is altogether damaged by the waves, and, besides this, other extrusions have grown on him, such as shellfish, seaweed, and stones; so that in every respect he resembles a marine creature, rather than what he naturally was. In such a condition do we not see the soul under a thousand evils? But this is where we ought, Glauco, to see it. In its love for wisdom, and to observe what it best attends, and what intimacies it affects, as being allied to that which is divine, immortal, and eternal. And also, what it would become, if it pursued wholly a quest of this kind, and was by this pursuit brought out of that sea of troubles in which it now rests. And when the stones and shellfish are shaken off, which at present, as they are mouldering on Earth, render its nature, in a great measure, earthy, stony, and savage. So these ailments prevent real happiness. And then might one behold its true nature, whether multiform, or uniform, and everything else concerning it.

'But we have, I think, sufficiently discussed its passions, and forms in human life. Have we not now discussed everything necessary in our reasoning, although we have not gained those rewards and honours of justice, as you say Hesiod and Homer have? But we find justice itself to be the highest reward for the soul; and that we should do what is just, whether we have or haven't got Gyges' ring on our finger, and, together with such a ring, the helmet of Pluto. Will it not now then, Glauco, be without envy, if, besides these prizes, we add those rewards to justice and the other virtues, which are bestowed on the soul by men and the Gods, both while the man is alive, and after he is dead?

'Now after our judgement is over, I demand again, on behalf of justice, that as you allow it to be highly esteemed, both by Gods and men. And that you allow it to have the same good reputation, so that it may also receive those prizes of victory, which it acquires from the reputation of good justice; and gives its blessing to those who possess it. Since it has already seemed to give those good gifts which arise from really being just, and that it does not deceive those who truly embrace it. Will you not then, in the first instance, grant me this? That it is not concealed from the Gods, what kind of man or woman any man or woman truly is? And if they are not hidden, one of them will be loved by the Gods, and one of them hated, as we agreed at the beginning. And shall we also agree that as to the man who is loved by the

Gods, that whatever comes to him from the Gods will be the very best possible, unless he has suffered some disastrous ill from his former depravity.

'We are then to reflect in this manner about the just man. If he happens to be in poverty, or in sickness, or in any other of those evils, these sufferings will yield him something good, either whether he is alive, or dead. For never at any time will he be neglected by the Gods who protect all those who earnestly endeavour to become just, and practise virtue as far as it is possible, for a man to resemble God.' 'It is reasonable, that such a man or woman should not be neglected by him whom he resembles. And are we not to think the opposite concerning the unjust man?' 'Yes. Such, then, would seem to be the prizes which the just man receives from the Gods.

'But what, do they receive from men? Is this not the case, if we are to discover the truth? Do not cunning and unjust men do the same as those athletes, who run well at the beginning, but not so well at the end? For at first they briskly leap forward, but in the end they appear ridiculous, with their ears drooping on their necks, and they run off without any prize. But such are the true athletes, who arriving at the end both receive the prizes, and are crowned with a wreath of laurels. Doesn't it happen similarly, for the most part, for the just man? At the end of every action and event of life they are both held in esteem, and receive rewards from their fellow men. I affirm now, that the just, when they are grown up, shall arrive at power if they desire magistracies, they shall marry happily when they wish, and shall settle their children in marriage agreeably to their hopes.

'And as for everything else you mentioned concerning the unjust, I now say concerning them, that on the other hand most of them, although they may be hidden while they are young, yet being caught at the end of life's race, will seem ridiculous. And when they become old, will be ridiculed, and in their wretchedness will be despicably treated both by foreigners and fellow citizens, and they may afterwards be tortured, and burnt, which you said were cruel punishments, and you spoke the truth. Imagine, you hear from me, that they suffer all this hell. Such as these are the prizes, the rewards and the gifts, which a just man receives in his lifetime, both from the Gods and men, besides those blessings which justice contains in itself.' 'And they are extremely beautiful, and likewise permanent.' 'Yes. But these consequences are nothing in number or magnitude, when compared with those which await each of the two at death.

'All this must be heard, that each of them may completely receive what is their due as a result of their effort in reasoning. However, I will not,' said I, 'tell you about the apologue of Alcinous, but only that of a very brave man called Er, the son of Armenius, by descent a Pamphylian, who happened to die in battle. When the dead were carried off after the tenth day, all bodies seemed to be corrupted; he was lifted up, and carried home. As he was about to be buried on the twelfth day, when laid out on the funeral pile, he revived; and being revived, he told them all that he had witnessed in the other state. He said that after his soul left the body, it journeyed with many others, and that they came to a certain dæmoniacal, supernatural place not of this world, where there were two chasms in the Earth, near to each other, and two other openings in the heavens opposite them, and judges sat between these chasms. That when they gave their judgement, they commanded the just to go on their right hand, and upwards through the heaven, fixing before them accounts of the judgement that had been pronounced. But the unjust they commanded to go to the left and downwards, and these also carried the records of all they had done.

'But when Er came before the judges, they ordered him to be a messenger to mankind concerning what took place there, and they commanded him to hear, and to contemplate everything that was in that place. He said that he saw there, through two openings, one of heaven, and one of Earth. The departed souls were judged there. Through the two openings he saw, rising through the one, out of the Earth, souls full of squalidness and dust. And through the other, he saw other souls descending pure, from heaven, and that on their arrival they seemed as if they had come from a long journey. They gladly went to rest themselves in a meadow, as in a public assembly, and saluted those with whom they were acquainted. And those who rose out of the Earth asked the others about the heaven above, while those from heaven asked them about the Earth below.

'These souls told one another, wailing and weeping about what they called to mind, and how much they had suffered, and all that they had seen in their journey under the Earth. It was a journey of a thousand years. And those souls from heaven explained their enjoyments, and spectacles of immense beauty. To narrate many of them to you, Glauco, would take much time. But this, Er said, was the gist; that whatever unjust actions any had committed, and how many they had injured, they were punished for all these separately tenfold, and that it was for each unjust action, a sentence of one hundred years. The life of a man being considered as so long that they must suffer tenfold punishment for the injustices they had done. So that if any had been the cause of many deaths, either by betraying cities or armies, or bringing men into slavery, or being confederates in any other wickedness, for each of these they reaped tenfold sufferings. And if, again, they had benefited any by good deeds, and had been just and holy, they were rewarded according to their deserts.

'Of those who died very young, and lived but a little time, it was not worth relating. But for impiety and piety towards the Gods and parents, and of homicide, he told them about more remarkable retributions. For he said he was present when one was asked by another, where the great Aridæus was? This Aridæus had been a Tyrant in a certain city of Pamphylia, a thousand years before, and had killed his aged father, and his elder brother, and had done many other evil deeds. The one who was asked replied that he neither comes here, nor will he ever come here. He also said that he witnessed other similar dreadful spectacles.

'He said that when we were near the mouth of the opening, and were about to ascend after having suffered everything else, we saw Aridaeus all of a sudden, and others, most of whom were Tyrants, and some private persons who had committed great iniquity. All of them who when they imagined they were to ascend the mouth of the opening, that it would not admit them, but bellowed, when any of those who were so polluted with wickedness, or who had not been sufficiently punished, attempted to ascend. And then, said he, fierce men, and fiery to the sight, standing by, and understanding the bellowing, took them and led them apart including Aridæus and the rest, binding their hands and their feet, and, thrusting down their heads, and pulling off their skin, dragging them to an outer road, and letting them be torn by thorns.

'They declared to those who passed by, on what account they had suffered these torments, and that they were being carried to be thrown into Tartarus. And so, he said, that in the midst of all their various terrors, this terror surpassed them all, lest the mouth should bellow, and that when it was silent everyone gladly ascended. And that the punishments and torments were such as these, and their rewards were the opposite of these. He also added that everyone, after they had been seven days in the meadow, when rising from there, it was necessary for them to depart on the eighth day, and arrive at another place on the fourth day after that; when they saw from above, through the whole of the heavens and the Earth, a light extended as a pillar, resembling the rainbow, but even more splendid and pure, at which they arrived after one day's journey.

'There they perceived, through the middle of the light from heaven, the extremities of its boundaries were extended, as this light was the belt of heaven, like the undergirding of warships, keeping the whole circumference united. He also saw that from the extremities, the spindle of Destiny was extended, by which revolutions were turned, and whose shaft and point were both of steel, but its wheel was combined with this and other hard substances. The nature of the wheel was of such a shape, like any wheel we see here. But you must conceive it, from what he said, to be of such a kind as if enclosed in some greater wheel, hollow and scooped out. There was another, but lesser wheel within it, adapted to it, like casks fitting one within another, and in the same way a third, and a fourth, and four more. So that the wheels were eight in all, as circles one within another, having their rims appearing upwards, and forming around the spindle one united convexity of one wheel, so that the shaft was driven through the middle of the eight. And the first and outermost wheels had the widest circumference at the rim. And the sixth had the second widest, and the fourth, the third widest, and the fourth widest was that of the eighth, and the fifth widest was that of the seventh, the sixth widest that of the fifth, and the seventh widest that of the third, and the eighth widest that of the second.

'Also the circle of the largest was variegated, and that of the seventh was the brightest, and that of the eighth took its colour from a reflection of the seventh. The second and fifth resembled each other, but were more yellow than the rest. But the third had the whitest colour, the fourth was reddish. The second, in whiteness surpassed the sixth, so that the shaft must turn round in a circle with all that it carries. And while the whole is turning round, the seven inner circles are gently turned round in a contrary motion to the whole. Again, of these, the eighth moves the swiftest; and next to it, and equal to one another, the seventh, the sixth, and the fifth, and the fourth went in a motion which appeared to them to have completed its circle in the third degree of swiftness. The fourth, in swiftness was the third, and the fifth was the second. And the spindle was turned round on the knees of Destiny.

'And on each of its circles there was seated a siren on the upper side, carried round, and singing with one voice, variegated by diverse modulations. And the whole of them, being eight, composed one harmony. There were another three sitting round, at equal distance one from another, each on a throne, the daughters of Necessity, the Fates, in white vestments, and having crowns on their heads. These were Lachesis, and Clotho, and Atropos, singing to the harmony of the sirens; Lachesis singing about the past,

Clotho the present, and Atropos the future. And that Clotho, at certain intervals, with her right hand laid hold of the spindle, and along with her mother turned round the outer circle. And Atropos, in like manner, turned the inner ones with her left hand. And Lachesis touched both of these, several times, with either hand.

'After they arrived here, it was necessary for them to go directly to Lachesis, where a certain prophet first of all ranged them in order, and afterwards drawing lots, the model of their lives, lay them on the knees of Lachesis, and ascending a lofty tribunal, he made a the speech to the virgin Lachesis, the daughter of Necessity, He said, "Souls of a day! This is the beginning of another period of men of mortal race. Fortune shall not receive you as you draw your lot, so you shall choose your fortune. He who draws the first lot, let him first make choice of a life, to which he must of necessity adhere. Mother Virtue is independent, which every one shall take from, more or less, according to the degree that he honours or dishonours her. The responsibility is his who makes the choice, and God is blameless."

'Then when he had said these things, he threw on all of them the lots, and each took up the one which fell beside him, save himself, as it was not allowed for him to take one. And each, when he had taken one, saw what number he had drawn. After this he placed on the ground before them the models of lives, many more than those we see at present. And they were all different, for there were lives of all kinds of animals, and human. And that among these there were Tyrants too, some of them perpetual, and others destroyed in the middle of their greatness. There were also lives of famous men, renowned either for beauty of person and feature, for bodily strength and skill in games, or else for high birth and the merits of ancestors. And in the same way there were lives of undistinguished men, and likewise lives of celebrated and uncelebrated women.

'But no settled character of soul was included in them, because with the change of life, the soul inevitably becomes changed itself. But in every other respect the materials were very variously combined, wealth appearing here, and poverty there, disease here, and health there, and here and there again, a mean between these extremes. This, my dear Glauco, is apparently the crucial moment when everything is at stake for a man, and for this reason, above all others, it is the duty of each of us diligently to investigate and study, to the neglect of every other subject, that science which may happily enable a man to learn and discover, who will instruct him, so as to be able to discriminate between a good and an evil life; and, according to his means to choose, always and everywhere, that better life, by carefully calculating the influence of all that was just mentioned, in combination or in separation, having a bearing upon the real excellence of a life.

'And he must consider who will teach him to understand what evil and good is brought about by excellence tempered with poverty or wealth, and how the result is affected by the state of soul, which enters into combination with it. And what are the consequences of blending together such ingredients as high or humble birth, private or public life, bodily strength or weakness, readiness or slowness of apprehension, and everything else of the kind, whether naturally belonging to the soul or accidentally acquired by it? So as to be able to form a judgement from all these combined data and, with an eye steadily fixed on the nature of the soul, to choose between the good and the evil life. Giving the name of evil to the life which will draw the soul into becoming more unjust, and the name of good to the life which will lead it to becoming more just, and bidding farewell to every other consideration.

'For we have seen that in life and in death it is best to choose between the two. With iron resolution we must hold fast to this opinion when we enter the future world, in order that there, as well as here, we may escape being dazzled by wealth and similar evils and may never plunge into usurpation or other corresponding courses of action, to the inevitable detriment of others, and to our own still heavier affliction. But we must know how to select that life which always steers a middle course between such extremes, and to shun excess on either side to the best of our ability, not only in this life, but also in that which is to come. For, by so acting, we are sure to become the most happy of men!

'To go back, the messenger from the other world reported that on the same occasion the interpreter spoke to this effect saying, "Even the last comer, if he chooses with discretion and lives strenuously, will find in store for him a life that is anything but bad, with which he may well be content." Let not the first choose carelessly, or the last despair." As soon as he had said these words, the one who had drawn the first lot advanced, and chose the most absolute despotism he could find, for so thoughtless was he, and greedy, that he had not carefully examined every point before making his choice, so that he failed to remark that he was fated therein, amongst other calamities, to devour his own children. Therefore, when he had studied all, at his leisure, he began to beat his breast and wailed about his choice, and, disregarding the previous admonitions of the interpreter, he laid the blame of his misfortune not upon himself, but upon Fortune and Destiny, and upon anybody sooner than himself. He was one of those who had come from heaven, and had lived during his former life under a well-ordered State constitution, and hence a measure of virtue had fallen to his share through the influence of habit, unaided by philosophy.

'Indeed, according to Er's account, more than half the persons similarly deluded, had come from heaven, which is to be explained by the fact that they had never endured the marvellous discipline of trouble. For, the majority of those who came from the Earth did not make their choice in this careless manner, because they had known affliction themselves, and had seen it in others. On this account, and also through the chances of the drawn lot, most of the souls exchanged an evil destiny for a good one, or a good destiny for an evil one. But if a man were always to study wisdom soundly, whenever he entered upon his career on Earth, and if it fell to his lot to choose anywhere but the very last, there is every probability, to judge by the account brought from the other world, that he would not only be happy while on Earth, but also that he would travel from this world to the other and back again, not along a rough and subterranean route, but along a smooth and heavenly road.

'It was a truly wonderful sight, he said, to watch how each soul selected its life, a sight at once melancholy, and ludicrous, and strange. The experience of their former life generally guided their choice. So he saw the soul which had once been that of Orpheus, choosing the life of a swan, because, from having been put to death by women, he detested the whole race so much that he would not consent to be conceived and born of a woman. And he saw the soul of Thamyras choosing the life of a nightingale. He saw also a swan changing its nature, and selecting the life of a man, and its example was followed by other animals.

'The soul that drew the twentieth lot chose a lion's life. It was the soul of Ajax the son of Telamon, who shrank from becoming a man because he recollected the decision respecting the arms of Achilles. He was followed by the soul of Agamemnon, who had been also taught by his sufferings to hate mankind so bitterly that he adopted, in exchange, an eagle's life. The soul of Atalanta, which had drawn one of the middle lots, held the great honours attached to the life of an athlete, and could not resist the temptation of taking it up. Then he saw the soul of Epeus the son of Panopeus, assuming the nature of a skilful working woman. And in the distance, among the last, he saw the soul of the buffoon Thersites putting on the exterior of an ape.

'It so happened that the soul of Odysseus had drawn the last lot of all. When he came up to choose, the memory of his former sufferings had so abated his ambition, that he sat about a long time looking for a quiet retired life, which with great trouble he discovered lying around, and thrown contemptuously aside by the others. As soon as he saw it, he chose it gladly, and said that he would have done the same, if he had even drawn the first lot. In like manner some of the other animals passed into men, and into one another; the unjust passing into the wild, and the just into the tame, so that every kind of mixture ensued. Now, when all the souls had chosen their lives in the order of the lots, they advanced in their turn to Lachesis, who dispatched with each of them the Destiny he had selected, to guard his life and satisfy his choice. This Destiny first led the soul to Clotho in such a way as to pass beneath her hand and the whirling motion of the distaff, and thus ratified the fate which each had chosen in the order of precedence. After touching her, the same Destiny led the soul next to the spinning wheel of Atropos, and so rendered the doom of Clotho irreversible.

'From there the souls passed straight forward under the throne of Destiny. When the rest had passed through it, Er himself also passed through, and they all travelled into the plain of Forgetfulness, through dreadfully suffocating heat, the ground being destitute of trees and all vegetation. As the evening came on, they took up their quarters by the bank of the river of Indifference, whose water cannot be held in any vessel. All persons are compelled to drink a certain quantity of the water; but those who are not preserved by prudence drank more than their quantity, and each, as he drank, forgets everything. When they had gone to rest, and it was now midnight, there was a clap of thunder and an earthquake, and in a moment the souls were carried up to their birth, this way and that, like shooting stars. Er himself was prevented from drinking any of the water; but how, and by what road, he reached his body, he knew not, only he knew that he suddenly opened his eyes at dawn, and found himself laid out upon the funeral pyre.

'And so, Glauco, this allegorical record was preserved, and did not perish; and it may also preserve us, if we will listen well to its warnings. In which case we shall pass prosperously across the river of Lethe, and not defile our souls. Indeed, if we follow my advice, believing the soul to be immortal, and to possess the power of entertaining all evil, as well as all good, we shall ever hold fast to the upward road, and devotedly cultivate justice combined with wisdom; so that we may be truly loved by one another, and by the Gods; not only during our stay on Earth, but also when, like conquerors in the games collecting the presents of their admirers, we receive the prizes of virtue. So that in both this life and during the journey of a thousand years which we have described, we may never cease to prosper! So be it, my friends, now you all fully understand, by this allegorical tale, the true meaning of justice.